Contents

1 Doctrine—The Foundation for Faith 5
2 The Salvation of Man 16
3 Teaching the Truths of Salvation 33
4 The Promised Holy Spirit 46
5 Teaching Students About the Holy Spirit 62
6 The Provision of Divine Healing 71
7 Teaching the Truths of Divine Healing 84
8 The Glorious Hope of His Coming 92
9 Teaching the Truths of the Second Coming 106
10 The Church—Doctrine on Display 115
Suggested Reading 127

ZENAS J. BICKET

WE HOLD THESE TRUTHS

GOSPEL PUBLISHING HOUSE
SPRINGFIELD, MISSOURI
02-0631

WE HOLD THESE TRUTHS

This is a Workers Training Division textbook. Credit for its study will be issued under Classification 3, Sunday School Department, Assemblies of God. A teacher's guide for group study with this book is available from the Gospel Publishing House. Order number 31-0878.

Library of Congress Catalog Card Number 78-56133
International Standard Book Number 0-88243-631-7
Printed in the United States of America

1

Doctrine—The Foundation for Faith

Doctrine is what the doctor teaches. Such a statement is meaningless today, though it would have made sense 700 years ago. At that time, the word *doctor* still meant a learned man or a teacher. A medical doctor (M.D.) is really a learned man in medicine.

What Is Doctrine?

Since the word *doctrine* comes from the same Latin word that gives us the word *doctor*, doctrine literally means something taught, or teaching and instruction. Christian doctrine is the system of fundamental Biblical truths arranged in a systematic form. As we study the entire Bible to determine all that it says about a particular subject, and as we arrange those Biblical statements into a comprehensive statement on a subject, we arrive at the important subjects of Christian doctrine:

Christology (the doctrine of Christ)
Pneumatology (the doctrine of the Holy Spirit)
Anthropology (the doctrine of man)
Soteriology (the doctrine of salvation)
Ecclesiology (the doctrine of the Church)
Angelology (the doctrine of angels)
Eschatology (the doctrine of last things)

In each word, the *-ology* ending means a branch of learning or instruction.

These and other doctrines are treated in great detail in theological textbooks which sometimes extend to many volumes. The scope of this book, however, is not all the doctrines of the Bible, but the ones most important to evangelical Pentecostals. There are four that stand out as the cardinal doctrines of the Assemblies of God:

Salvation through the work of Jesus Christ
The Holy Spirit and His work in Christians
Divine Healing as part of the atonement
The Second Coming of Jesus Christ

Some of these doctrines are also held by other groups of Christians; some are distinctively Pentecostal. But they are the most important of all the doctrines for our daily lives.

Doctrine, Theology, and Religion

Doctrine is teaching. A specific doctrine is the collected learning on a given subject. Theology means literally "the study of God" or our knowledge of God and His relations with man. So *doctrine* and *theology* are closely related words, sometimes used interchangeably.

Whereas doctrine or theology is knowledge about God, *religion* is the practical application of theology. For the Christian, it is the complete system of beliefs, practices, and ethical values by which he lives. Unfortunately, a person's doctrine (what he professes to believe) and his religion (the practical demonstration of what he truly believes) are sometimes inconsistent. But the way a man lives is a better indicator of what he believes than the lip service he gives to a doctrinal or theological system.

The Great Need for Doctrinal Study

Many young people lack any systematic knowledge of the Bible and its doctrines. Even those who have attended Sunday school consistently frequently look on the Bible as a collection of stories repeated by Sunday school teachers in order to emphasize some moral or ethical principle. Interspersed between these well-known stories are some memory verses and long, dull passages which only preachers attempt to read.

Evidence of this lack of a systematic understanding of the Bible and its doctrines is seen in the results of some simple surveys conducted on young people who have had some exposure to Bible teaching. What do the following actual responses reveal about the Biblical knowledge level of the high-school-age students who gave the answers?

"His name shall be called . . . the *(Justice)* of Peace" (Isaiah 9:6).

Jesus was baptized by *(Moses)*.

Jesus was in agony in the Garden of *(Eden)*.

"Ye seek Jesus . . . He is not here: for he is *(dead)*" (Matthew 28:5, 6).

"Charity" in the King James Version of 1 Corinthians 13 is now taken to mean *(give)*.

"I have fought a *(losing)* fight . . . I have kept the faith" (2 Timothy 4:7).

Jacob wrestled all night with *(insomnia)*.

The wise sayings in Proverbs are generally attributed to *(parents)*.

Of even greater concern than the deficiency of young people in Biblical and doctrinal knowledge is the same weakness in Sunday school teachers and workers. In a special evaluation project, the Fundamentals for Sunday School Workers Equivalency Testing Program, the national Sunday School Department of the Assemblies of God conducted testing of workers. Less than 50 percent demonstrated the necessary knowledge of the Sunday school and its teaching ministry! And less than 25 percent demonstrated the more essential grasp of the content that is to be taught! Is it any wonder that the youth give evidence of deficiency in Bible and doctrinal knowledge?

Similar deficiencies could no doubt be demonstrated in the Sunday school teachers of most church groups in our country. But we should take no comfort in belonging to a poorly informed majority, especially in matters of such importance as Bible knowledge and the understanding of doctrine. The Assemblies of God as a denomination is built on the strong affirmation that the Bible is God's inspired revelation that shows man the way of salvation and righteous living. Our teachers should be better informed on the content they teach than the results of the FSSW Equivalency Testing Program indicate.

Some may feel that anyone can teach a Sunday school class because the needed material is contained in the teacher's quarterly for each lesson. But the teacher's background knowledge should go far beyond the limited focus of each lesson. Each teacher should give diligence to becoming a classroom workman who needs not to be ashamed of his understanding of God's Word and can rightly divide the word of truth (2 Timothy 2:15).

The subject of this book, a survey of the cardinal doctrines of the Assemblies of God, has been prayerfully selected because of a demonstrated need and a desire to help the many dedicated Sunday school teachers who want to do a better job for the kingdom of God. Although you will not know all that can be known about Biblical doctrine when you finish your study of this book, careful attention to its content will make you a much better workman for God than you have been. We all want to be stamped with that divine seal, "Approved Unto God."

The Value of Biblical Doctrine

How important is a proper understanding of doctrine? Wouldn't it be easier to leave the teaching to other Christians than to give all the time and effort necessary to understand and explain the major doctrinal truths in the Bible? And if some people attend Bible college for 3 or 4 years to study the Bible and its doctrines, what chance does the worker without this opportunity have?

The privilege of studying God's Word and His work in every area of human life can be a real blessing. But most of the great men and women God has used throughout history have come to know an intimate relationship with God and an understanding of His Word in spite of a lack of formal classroom training. The classroom does not make a student. A desire to learn and a commitment to study with the Great Teacher is all it takes. But whether or not we serve as Sunday school teachers, every Christian has an overwhelming reason for making the understanding of doctrine a major goal.

Doctrine Is the Test of Discipleship

Jesus said to a group of His disciples: "If you hold to my teaching, you are really my disciples. Then you will know the truth, and the truth will set you free" (John 8:31, 32, *NIV*).

On the seal of some colleges and universities are the words, "Ye shall know the truth, and the truth shall make you free." The meaning of the verse, according to some educators, is that sufficient knowledge will liberate people from all those things that make life an unhappy experience.

This reasoning takes the verse out of context. Verse 31 must be read along with verse 32 because of the connecting word (translated "and" or "then"). Jesus was saying that only disciples really know the truth—the truth that will set them free. And the way to be a disciple is through obedience to the teachings, or doctrine, of Christ.

So doctrine is important. It is the teaching of God, through His Son and through the inspired writers of the Old and New Testaments. Certainly, we must obey the doctrine delivered to us, but we cannot obey it completely unless we first understand it. Hearing or understanding comes by and through the Word (Romans 10:17).

Doctrine Is a Safeguard Against Error

Our eternal salvation could depend on our understanding of Biblical doctrine. Peter warned against false teachers who out of greed will exploit unsettled Christians with fictitious stories (2 Peter 2:3) and beguile unstable souls with their deception (v. 14). Man in his blindness and disobedience has fashioned wrong conceptions about God. These errors take on the form of paganism, humanism, or doctrinal departures from the truth of Scripture.

It is not true that all religions will lead to heaven, just so long as the seeker is sincere. Error in doctrine could lead us away from God rather than toward Him. Our doctrine must be solidly based on the Bible.

Doctrine Is the Basis for Our Conduct and Service

Strong doctrinal beliefs are essential for the full development of strong Christian character. The stronger the belief, the more dependable and upright the character will be. If we want our children to grow up to be men and women of character and integrity, we must fervently plant in their minds and hearts the teachings and doctrines of God's Word.

We cannot share our faith meaningfully until we can tell others about it. And unless we can relate our spiritual experience to the pattern described in Scripture and promised by God to all men and women, we have little to impart to others. "Always be prepared to give . . . the reason for the hope that you have" (1 Peter 3:15, *NIV*). This preparation requires that we study the Bible and the doctrines it provides for us.

The Search for Doctrinal Certainties

Man has always sought for a system to explain his existence and the world around him. He has attempted to find or to make a standard by which he can live in a community of other people like himself. Through the centuries he has tried various avenues unsuccessfully.

Natural Law Is Not the Standard

From nature, some men have reasoned, we can derive a system of ethics without consulting the Bible or any other Christian revelation. According to Romans 2:13, 14, however, natural law serves only to condemn the sinner and direct him to Christ as the Creator of nature. It cannot serve independently as a substitute for God's revealed law.

Human Philosophy Is Not the Standard

Men have tried to elevate reason as a standard of ethics and conduct. They have attempted to define good and evil in terms that omit God and Satan as the primary antagonists in the battle for the control of man's destiny.

Some philosophers have even said that each man is a rule or standard unto himself and he needs no external guide for belief or practice. But human philosophy as doctrine has led the world exactly nowhere.

God's Word Is the True Doctrine

"All Scripture is given by inspiration of God, and is profitable for doctrine, for reproof, for correction, for instruction in righteousness: that the man of God may be perfect, thoroughly furnished unto all good works" (2 Timothy 3:16, 17). Pentecostals have been known, and must continue to be known, as people of the Bible.

The Inspired and Inerrant Word of God

The Bible is different from all other books. It is the only book in the world that is wholly inspired by God. The Holy Spirit of God is the divine Author of the Bible: "For the prophecy came not in old time by the will of man: but holy men of God spake as they were moved by the Holy Ghost" (2 Peter 1:21).

This divine inspiration extends equally and fully to all parts of the 66 Books—the historical and poetical as well as the doctrinal and prophetical. Every word is inspired and without error in the original manuscripts; because of many copyings and translations, a few minor inaccuracies have appeared in the translations. No vital doctrine has been affected, however, by these variations. Some of them are being cleared up by recent discoveries of older manuscripts.

Conflict Over Biblical Inerrancy

One of the most important conflicts among evangelicals in recent years concerns the inerrancy of the Scriptures.

Some have called it "The Battle for the Bible," believing strongly that the acceptance of even the smallest error in the Bible begins a process that ultimately will destroy the very foundation of our Christian faith and experience. If we cannot trust even the most minute facts of Scripture, how can we be sure that the important truths on which our faith is built are dependable?

Inerrant means "free from error." It is generally used as a synonym for *infallible,* which means "incapable of error." The Statement of Fundamental Truths of the Assemblies of God calls the Bible "the infallible rule of faith and conduct . . . superior to conscience and reason." Like the doctrinal statements of other evangelical groups, the Statement of Fundamental Truths does not use the word *inerrant.*

Some younger evangelical scholars, many influenced by views taught at nonevangelical seminaries, have taken advantage of this omission to advocate a position that is contrary to the intent of the original statement. Because of apparent difficulties in Scripture (especially in chronology and historical fact), they maintain that some sections of the Bible are not without error even though they are still inspired. Others retain the word *inerrant* but stretch its meaning through a redefinition of terms.

But inerrancy, in its straight dictionary definition, is absolutely essential if the Church is to retain its vitality and supernatural distinctive.

The Importance of the Doctrine of Inerrancy

The Bible is God's Word to sinful man. God himself must be true and infallible, without error. The word He speaks must likewise be infallible or without error. To agree that there is error in God's Word is to cast doubt on the very character of God.

To believe that the original Word of God had error in it, just because man had a part in recording it in written form, is to deny the full meaning of inspiration and reduce the Bible to the level of any highly moral book written by a human being.

Some critics of the inerrancy doctrine will accept infallibility in "matters of faith and practice" but deny it in matters of science or history. Although the Bible is not a science textbook, it records scientific fact with the same infallible authority with which it treats doctrine and practice. Unless we accept this view we are faced with another problem: Whose decision determines what parts of the Bible are true and what parts are in error?

Some opponents of inerrancy claim that evangelicals worship a Book rather than the Christ who is portrayed in the Book. They further maintain that Christians should place ultimate authority in Christ, not in the Bible as a dated record of God's dealings in the past. But we have no other way of knowing about Jesus Christ and His authority apart from the Bible. If the Book that reveals Christ to us is subject to error, then it may not be describing the Saviour as the human-divine Being that He is. The whole framework of Christian faith rests on the inerrancy of the Scriptures.

You Can Trust God's Word

We cannot deny that there are some unanswered questions concerning the Bible and its historical, chronological, and scientific statements. But there have been enough answers uncovered for previously unsolved problems to assure us that we can trust God's Word, knowing that when all the explanations have been revealed, the inspired Word will stand true and without error.

Unfortunately, there are "scholars" who, in the face of unanswered questions, choose to place their trust in man's fallible mind rather than in the inerrant Word of an infallible God. The reliability of the Bible has been proven beyond any reasonable doubt. The unreliability and limited scope of man's reason, on the other hand, has been proven with the same consistency.

Satan is battling hard in these last days to discredit the inspired Word. But you must settle this point in your mind—without any wavering—before your study of the remainder of this textbook will have any value to you personally or to the students you may instruct as a teacher. God's Word is inspired, it is infallible, and it is inerrant. You can, and you must, trust it!

2

The Salvation of Man

Cardinal Doctrine One

The story of salvation is simple; even a child can understand it. In spite of its simplicity, some of the greatest intellects of the world have failed to understand it. They have called it foolishness. The message of salvation "is to them that perish, foolishness; but unto us which are saved, it is the power of God" (1 Corinthians 1:18).

What makes the difference? Why is salvation a powerful reality for some but a foolish myth for others? The answer lies in the set of mind that we bring to this thrilling story of God reaching down to receive sinful man. Blinded by pride, some men proclaim the strength and sufficiency of the human mind. There is no need for a god when men boast of the technology, culture, and society that human hands have fashioned. To Madalyn Murray O'Hair and her atheistic cohorts, the message of salvation is foolish and absurd.

The story of salvation is simple if you really believe three basic assumptions. First, *God is.* The person who struggles with this foundational truth will find that the message of the Cross is little more than interesting reading. The Bible speaks eloquently of the presence of God in human history, but it never once attempts to prove that God exists. "In the beginning God . . ." (Genesis 1:1).

That's the extent of the proof. "He that cometh to God must believe that he is" (Hebrews 11:6). Reading the Word will confirm what we have already accepted by faith, but it will not through logic persuade the atheist of God's existence.

Second, the story of salvation is simple if one believes that God has revealed himself and His plan of salvation through the Holy Bible, the inspired and infallible Word of God to mankind. When men use human wisdom and reasoning to bring the Word down to the level of man-made literature, and they judge it to contain errors of fact, they make the plan of salvation very difficult for those who need to know the Saviour.

Third, the story of salvation is simple if one believes that Jesus is the divine Son of God who willingly came to earth to die as a sacrifice that our sins might be forgiven. If Jesus was only a man, His death has no more significance than that of any other man. But the death of a virgin-born, God-in-the-flesh Saviour would make a difference.

To doubt that God exists, to doubt that the Bible is His special and inspired Word to men and women, or to doubt that Jesus was actually the Son of God—any one of these faithless acts will make the plan of salvation extremely difficult to understand and impossible to receive.

But faith is the foundation of salvation. "Without faith it is impossible to please him" (Hebrews 11:6). So our study of God's plan of salvation will be difficult or simple, depending on what you have done with these three basic assumptions.

A Perfect Creation

For man, the story of salvation must begin with a sinless and perfect creation. For an all-knowing God, the story begins even earlier. Christ was "foreordained before the foundation of the world" to be the sacrificial Lamb without blemish or spot (1 Peter 1:19, 20). God knew that Adam and Eve would lose the beautiful Garden of Eden and all the blessings it represented, so even before it happened He had a plan for restoring the broken relationship between God and man.

The Glory of God's Handiwork

Out of darkness, out of nothing, God brought into existence, by the Word of the Son, a dazzling, beautiful world. The light created by the first act of power provided a perfect backdrop for what was to follow. Another "let there be" rolled the moisture-laden heavens apart from the mass of water below. The third act of creation brought into existence the dry land which was to be so essential to human life. At the same time, plants and all forms of vegetation brought unimagined beauty to the stark earth. There were as yet no weeds to destroy the "good" creation.

Then God moved back through His beautiful but empty spaces and populated them with fantastic variety and wonderfully coordinated creatures. In the upper firmament or heavens He placed the life-sustaining sun and the moon and the stars. To inhabit the atmosphere He created all manner of bird life, and for the seas He made the fish and sea creatures. And in His crowning acts of creation, He brought movement and sound as He molded and breathed life into the animals and man. Imagine, if you can, the freshness and sparkle of that perfect creation, as yet untouched by the taint of sin!

Separating Fact From Fiction

Some people today hold a view that the world evolved from a chance beginning, over millions of years, without any intervention by an omnipotent God. This explanation of the beginning of things is called atheistic evolution. But this theory violates the first basic assumption—God is—and it makes the story of salvation incredibly difficult to believe and appropriate. If God did not begin it all, man has nowhere to turn for an escape from his sinful and lost condition.

Yet countless persons have chosen this fiction in preference to the fact. The theory of evolution has some advantages for rebellious men who do not want to recognize the claims of God on their lives. If man can persuade himself and those around him that there is no God who makes demands of us, he can escape, at least temporarily, the feelings of guilt and responsibility. But at the same time he closes the door of salvation, the only opportunity to flee from his sinful nature, both in this life and in the eternal hereafter. God is! And He made everything!

The Importance of Adam and Eve

Some persons look on the creation-evolution debate as an unnecessary disagreement between the unrelated areas of theology and science. Maybe, they reason, God chose the process of evolution as His means of creation; if this were true, Christians could live comfortably with a foot on each side of the fence. But the existence of an Adam and an Eve, two distinct individuals, is crucial to the reasonableness and power of God's plan of salvation.

Paul made the matter strikingly clear: "For since by man came death, by man came also the resurrection of the dead. For as in Adam all die, even so in Christ shall all be made alive" (1 Corinthians 15:21, 22). Jeremiah stated the fact of original or inborn sin: "The heart is deceitful above all things, and desperately wicked" (Jeremiah 17:9).

All men are born under this spiritual and moral handicap because Adam, the father of the race, sinned and brought the penalty into the basic nature of all men. Original sin, with its universal effect on all descendants, could not be explained by an evolutionary line of creatures that evolved into a multitude of races.

The first Adam and the second Adam (Christ) were both distinct individuals. Without that fact, salvation as the remedy for the completely sinful nature of man would be meaningless. The theology of salvation, as stated in the New Testament, demands the special creation of Adam and Eve.

Made in the Image of God

God made man that he might bring glory to God (Ephesians 1:12). He made His crowning creation perfect in body, soul, and spirit. By virtue of his creation by God, Adam was a son of God. Unlike the animal creation, Adam and Eve possessed reason and moral awareness. They knew right from wrong. The divine likeness in human form was a rich treasure in a temple of clay. But the perfect work was soon marred by the blot of sin.

The Fall and Its Effect

What if Adam and Eve had never sinned? The mind struggles to comprehend what life might be like today if sin had never entered our world. But such speculation is wasted. We must live with the reality.

Rebellion as the Origin of Sin

Where did it all begin? Adam blamed Eve. Eve blamed the serpent. The serpent might have blamed Satan for overpowering his beautiful physical form. But Satan was originally an angel. Who or what tempted him while he was still in heaven?

These are difficult questions on which the Bible is noticeably silent. But there is no doubt about the reality of sin. We can only recount the story of Satan's fall and speculate briefly how it might have begun.

Although there has been some disagreement on the interpretation of Ezekiel 28 and Isaiah 14, there is fairly common agreement among evangelicals that the passages have a twofold application: (1) the historical kings of Tyre and Babylon, and (2) the pride and fall of Lucifer (Satan). Satan is not mentioned by name in Ezekiel, but the description moves at times beyond any possible human applications: "Perfect in beauty" (Ezekiel 28:12); "Thou hast been in Eden" (v. 13); "Thou art the anointed cherub" (v. 14); and, "Thou wast perfect in thy ways from the day that thou wast created, till iniquity was found in thee" (v. 15). These certainly look beyond any human figure.

Isaiah 14:12-14 more directly mentions Lucifer. Sin began with pride. Lucifer said, "I will be like the Most High" (v. 14). From that rebellious beginning grew conflict and open warfare against Almighty God. Other angels joined the rebellion and became the wicked spirits who assist Satan in his diabolic opposition to God's kingdom of righteousness.

The Fall of Adam and Eve

Satan was unable to wrest the control of heaven from God. Fallen from that glorious beginning, he sought a battleground on which he could express his defiance. The perfect creation which God had so recently completed became the arena in which he attempted to do what he had not been able to do in heaven.

Was God less able to defeat Satan on earth after He had

so totally banished him from heaven? There is no doubt that God could have destroyed Satan, leaving him no opportunity to tempt and afflict the creatures of His making. But God never loses control of events, either in human history or in the spirit world. Just as He makes the wrath or evil of men to praise His name (Psalm 76:10), so He turned the rebellion of Satan to His own purpose: to prove the voluntary love and obedience of His children. Having fallen from his perfect state as an angel in heaven, Satan became an adversary and deceiver. But God has never relinquished His authority and power.

The story of the first sin of Adam and Eve need not be recited here. Genesis 3 recounts it in detail. The thing that is important is that Adam and Eve were created with all they needed to remain free from sin. They knew right from wrong and possessed the powers of reason and understanding. The command of God was not beyond their comprehension. They were given dominion over the earth; their fall was not caused by fear or weakness. Just as Satan was accountable for his pride and disobedience, so Adam and Eve had to answer for their rebellion.

The Results of the Fall

Every act in our lives has some consequence. But no act of any human being has had the consequence of the first disobedience of Adam and Eve. Sin ruined everything. All of physical creation felt the effect of the curse. Toil, sorrow, sickness, and death came to afflict the human race. Adam and Eve became aware of their guilt and separation from God. This has been the natural order of things since that original sin brought evil into man's world.

Furthermore, the divine image in man was marred

even though it was not lost entirely. All persons since Adam and Eve have been born as sinners and have been guilty of committing actual sin. "For all have sinned, and come short of the glory of God" (Romans 3:23). The ideal relationships that God had intended should exist among all of His children were shattered by inner discord and outward conflict. The removal of these spiritual and moral handicaps is what the plan of salvation is all about.

The Nature of Sin

Sin is ugly. Satan sometimes disguises it to make it appear more attractive, but when we see it as it really is, as God sees it, it is repulsive and vile. Solomon knew this. He wrote: "There is a way that seemeth right unto a man; but the end thereof are the ways of death" (Proverbs 16:25).

Sin can be summed up in one phrase: rebellion against God. Several Greek words are translated as *sin* in the New Testament. They can also be translated as "failure to hit the mark," "failure to listen when God speaks," "going beyond a permitted boundary," "stumbling or falling down," "an error caused by ignorance of what one should have known," "to be overcome or defeated," and "ungodliness or outright evil." But at the root of each of these definitions is the fact that sin—whether failure, falling, error, iniquity, or lawlessness—is against God and what He has asked of man.

God's Plan of Restoration

The situation we have been describing is bad. First there was the beauty of the original creation. But ugly sin belched its contamination like untreated sewage flowing into a beautiful fresh-water lake. Or, to use another comparison, Satan, like a bad boy, pushed that beautiful lamp of God's perfect creation off the table and onto the floor where it was smashed into thousands of pieces.

Some people see the plan of salvation as God's plastic bottle of *Elmer's Glue-All,* the means by which He sweeps up the shattered fragments and patiently and methodically glues the many pieces back together. But a repaired lamp is never as good as the original; these people dream with longing of what life would have been like if Adam and Eve had not sinned.

Yet God is and has always been in control. He is not a frustrated adult running around after Satan to pick up the pieces and salvage whatever He can of His perfect creation. No, He forces the wrath of Satan to bring praise to His name. The new creation produced by His plan of restoration is better than the original was in its perfect state. The new creature has been tested and declared a child of God; redeemed and filled with the grace and love of Christ himself. How much more He appreciates our worship, and how much more we can appreciate our Saviour, after we have been delivered from the bondage of sin.

A poet in the 14th century became so captivated by the excitement of his restored relationship with God that he wrote a poem called "Oh, Happy Sin." His theme was that he would never have known Jesus as his Saviour and special Friend if Adam and Eve had not sinned. No sin should ever be called happy or good, but the feelings of the poet should remind us that God has never been bested by Satan. What He has made available to us, both in this life and the next, as a result of His saving work, is a thrilling and magnificent blessing.

Divine Initiative

God does not force His salvation on anyone. He simply offers it to everyone. Because of this fact, some people have reasoned that anyone who does accept God's salvation has actually done something to save himself. Others say that God does it all and man has no choice; if God wants to save him, he will be saved whether he wants to be saved or not. Neither of these extreme positions is correct. Those who tend to give man a choice in his salvation have been called Arminians. Those who deny that man has any free will in the matter are called Calvinists.

The truth lies between the extremes. Many verses in the Bible speak of the choice that man must make. But his choice does not save him; it only allows God to save him. Salvation is a gift of God, "not of works, lest any man should boast" (Ephesians 2:9).

We sometimes describe the way in which a young couple will press through difficulties and hardship to establish a marriage and a home by saying, "Love finds a way." The same can be said of God. God's love for His creation, even after it had fallen, was so great "that he gave his only begotten Son" (John 3:16). God's plan of restoration grew out of His love. He took the initiative and reached out toward man. We must never forget this important truth.

The Divine Sacrifice

Why did the plan of restoration include a sacrifice? We cannot fully understand it, but God's Word declares that it had to be. "Without shedding of blood is no remission" (Hebrews 9:22). The same thing was said in the Old Testament, and the entire system of sacrifices was built on the fact. "For the life of the flesh is in the blood; . . . it is the blood that maketh an atonement for the soul" (Leviticus 17:11). Whereas the Jews had for centuries slaughtered and sacrificed animals as commanded by the

Law, Jesus, as the divine Son of God, was the perfect Sacrifice offered "once for all" (Hebrews 10:10).

Who is Jesus Christ, this Sacrifice for the sin of all mankind? He is the only begotten Son of God and also the Son of Man, since He came into the world by being born of the Virgin Mary. The first word of His name, *Jesus,* means Saviour (Matthew 1:21). The word *Christ* means "the Anointed One" or "the Messiah." He was both human and divine during His years on earth. His Father is our Heavenly Father, God himself. His mother was Mary.

With this parentage, Jesus was 100 percent human and 100 percent divine. This may seem like a paradox, but it simply means that we can identify with Him completely as a human being, knowing that He was just as human as we are, although He never sinned (Hebrews 4:15). At the same time, we can look to Him as the all-powerful, miracle-working Person of the divine Godhead, knowing that He is able and desires to use His divine power and authority to make us sons and daughters of God, conformed to His image.

The Work of Christ

Jesus performed many works during His life on earth, but they all pointed toward the one work for which He came to earth: to die for the sins of the world (John 1:29). His work in providing salvation or deliverance from sin includes His death, His resurrection, and His ascension. He not only had to die for us, He had to also rise again to prove His death was different from all others and that He was a living Person who could impart His divine life to us on a day-by-day basis. He not only had to rise from the dead for us, He had to also ascend to the right hand of the Father to make intercession for us.

The Death of Jesus Christ. The central event and doctrine for all Christians is the fact that "Christ died for our sins" (1 Corinthians 15:3). We speak of the four cardinal doctrines of the New Testament Church, but the other three are meaningless without this foundational one. It is *the cardinal doctrine* of the cardinal doctrines. The atoning death of Christ is the unique feature of the Christian religion.

At the fall of Adam and Eve, sin came like a giant obstacle to break the easy flow of communion between God and man. Man cannot remove the obstruction. If it is to be removed, God must do it. This He has done by sending His Son to carry the sin penalty that we should have carried. He accomplished for us what we were powerless to do for ourselves.

The Resurrection of Jesus Christ. Salvation through the death of Christ is an inward miracle. But the outward miracle, the great miracle on which Christianity rests, is the resurrection of Jesus Christ. Once the validity of this event is accepted, all the miracles of the Biblical record are believable and the miracle of salvation is authenticated. The entire Christian faith stands or falls on this central miracle of Christ's resurrection. The earthly life of Jesus ended, not with the question mark of death, but with the exclamation point of resurrection!

The evidences of the Resurrection are well established and dependable—except to the skeptic who determines before the evidence has been heard that he will not believe. The written sacred record is more reliable than all the other histories that have been written about the event from that day to the present. The tomb was empty. The precautions taken by the Romans to make sure that nothing improper was done to the body point faithfully to the reality of the Resurrection. The testimony of the disciples who saw Jesus after His resurrection is powerful evidence. It all adds up to one conclusion: Up from the grave He arose . . . a victor!

Because of the Resurrection, we know that Jesus is all that He claimed to be: the Son of God, our Saviour, our Lord. The death of Christ, coupled with His resurrection, constitute the atoning work of God.

The Ascension of Christ. Christ's entrance into the world was supernatural and so was His departure. But He did not just disappear. He ascended into heaven where He is now seated at the right hand of the Father (Romans 8:34). A living Intercessor makes our salvation just as current and alive today as it was when we first believed.

The Nature of Salvation

Christ's death and resurrection brought salvation to man. We have already seen that salvation means to be set free from sin and its penalty. But what actually takes place? A more complete understanding of salvation makes the reality of this divine work even more meaningful and precious to the Christian.

The sellers of diet foods and special formulas for losing weight frequently print "before" and "after" photographs to advertize their products. But no picture can capture the vast contrast between the sinner *before* salvation and the Christian *after* salvation. There are three words the Bible uses to describe this contrast: *regeneration, justification,* and *sanctification.*

Regeneration

The soul of sinful man, dead in trespasses and iniquity, needs a new life. This new and higher life is imparted at salvation by a divine act of regeneration. Regeneration is not the gaining of additional knowledge, moral or ethical improvement, being baptized in water, or joining a church. It is not something added to what we are. It is a complete change—an exchange of the old life for a new one.

The New Birth. In recent months it has become popular to speak of being "born again." When the term was first used by several public figures, some news reporters seemed at a loss to understand the meaning of this unfamiliar term. But it is one of the figures the Bible uses to emphasize the regeneration aspect of salvation (John 3:7). At salvation, each person becomes a child of God. This act of creative grace is truly a new birth. The term *adoption* (Galatians 4:5) is another figure used to describe our being brought into God's family at salvation.

A New Creature. Regeneration is the change wrought by the Spirit of God by which a person becomes a new creature in Jesus Christ. "If any man be in Christ, he is a new creature: old things are passed away; behold, all things are become new" (2 Corinthians 5:17). In saving us, God does not simply energize the old creation with new ability and power. The God who created man in the first place, only to see him fall into sin, recreates him at salvation by the operation of His Holy Spirit. The practical result is a radical change in the nature, character, desires, and motives of the transformed individual.

Justification

The word *justify* is a judicial term meaning to acquit, to declare righteous. At the moment of salvation, the guilty sinner stands before God, the righteous Judge; but instead of a sentence of condemnation, he receives a sentence of acquittal.

Justification deals with our relationship with God. It is not related to our personal righteousness or spiritual condition. It causes no one to be righteous. Rather, it is God's declaration that we are righteous, in spite of the sin and disobedience that filled our lives before the supernatural miracle of God's grace.

All sin is disobedience against God, and sin must be judged. But when sinful man comes to the Great Judge and asks forgiveness for his disobedience, the Judge says, "I declare you to be righteous." The past is forgiven and forgotten and man's relationship to God is restored to what it was intended to be before the Fall. All guilt, condemnation, and separation are removed by the act of justification. "Who shall lay any thing to the charge of God's elect? It is God that justifieth" (Romans 8:33).

Justification is more than pardon. A pardoned criminal is not regarded as being righteous. He is only pardoned from the penalty of his crime. But the Christian is declared righteous. Justification goes beyond forgiveness. Justification declares one to be righteous and then demonstrates toward the justified person an attitude that says, "You are just as righteous as if you had never sinned."

Sanctification

Another aspect of our salvation is sanctification. In regeneration we receive a new life and nature. In justification we receive a new standing: imputed righteousness. In sanctification we receive the spiritual life of Christ in our character and conduct.

Holiness is a synonym that helps us understand the meaning of sanctification. Whereas the justification aspect of salvation stresses that we have been declared righteous or holy, the sanctification aspect makes us holy.

Sanctification must be seen in its two applications. There is an instantaneous sanctification at the moment we become saved. But this does not mean we have arrived at the spiritual perfection God desires for each of His children. There is also a progressive life of sanctification which has its beginning at the moment of salvation. As in the act of instantaneous sanctification, the Holy Spirit is the primary Agent in helping us progressively to become like Jesus. His work of sanctification should be greatly accelerated when the believer remains filled with the Spirit after his baptism in the Holy Spirit. This work of sanctification will be discussed in a later chapter.

The basic meaning of the word *sanctify* is separation or being set apart. The Bible speaks of persons and places being sanctified or holy. They were set apart for God's possession and use. The 7th day was set apart for rest and worship. "God blessed the seventh day, and sanctified it" (Genesis 2:3). "Remember the sabbath day, to keep it holy" (Exodus 20:8). A house or a field could be sanctified (Leviticus 27:14-17). The Levites were separated (Numbers 8:14). At salvation, we are sanctified, consecrated, or set apart.

The other important meaning of sanctification is *purification*. The presence of the Holy Spirit in our hearts will purify our thoughts, desires, motives, and actions. God desires holiness to touch our entire being—body, soul, and spirit. The sanctification that comes at salvation permeates and affects every part of us. We are not only declared to be righteous, but we also begin to become the holy beings God desires us to be.

Other Aspects of Salvation

Regeneration, justification, and sanctification are three important aspects of salvation that make the meaning of the miracle clearer. There are other terms used in Scripture to shed light on what happens to us at salvation.

Atonement. The literal meaning is "the state of being 'at one' or in agreement with another." Usually applied to a sacrifice which removes sin and restores fellowship between God and man. (Romans 5:11. See also reconciliation.)

Assurance. The certainty which comes to the believer that God has accepted him and forgiven his sins (John 3:36; Romans 8:16; Hebrews 10:22).

Reconciliation. The restoration of relationship between two parties who formerly were enemies or hostile to one another (Romans 5:10, 11; 2 Corinthians 5:18-21; Ephesians 2:14-18; Colossians 1:19-22).

Redemption. Deliverance from some evil or bondage through the payment of a price. Jesus Christ is a Redeemer and His atoning work is described as redemption (Matthew 20:28; 1 Corinthians 6:20; Ephesians 1:7; 1 Peter 1:18, 19).

Repentance. Godly sorrow for sin with a sincere effort to forsake it (2 Corinthians 7:9, 10; 2 Peter 3:9).

* * * * *

What a glorious plan of salvation was devised by God. Through it we have been brought back into fellowship and right standing before Him. What a thrill to think of the great love that reached down and has lifted us out of our sin and seated us in heavenly places in Christ Jesus (Ephesians 2:6). "How shall we escape, if we neglect so great salvation . . .?" (Hebrews 2:3).

3

Teaching the Truths of Salvation

Cardinal Doctrine One

Dozens of rats roamed through the home of a self-employed chemist in a midwestern city. But the man wasn't the least bit upset. The rodents were "just like hamsters or gerbils," he said.

"There is a prejudice against the wild rat, the sewer rat," the chemist said. "But my rats are domesticated. They cause no trouble." The man claimed to be breeding a strain of tame rats with "the ability to relate to a person in a manner similar to a dog or cat."

The district judge, however, didn't agree with the strange views of the chemist. He ordered the "pet-keeper" to get rid of all but 24 of his dozens of rats—and to keep those in cages.

The story is almost unbelievable. Yet it was carried over the wires of a leading press service.

The majority of men and women today do things that are just as bizarre as the actions of the chemist. They try to make pets out of their sins. They attempt to make them respectable, the style, or the "in thing." But no amount of domestication or dressing up will change the basic nature of rats—or of sin.

As you teach the truths of salvation, you must never forget that sin is ugly. It always has been and it always will be.

Teaching Toward Vital Experience

In the natural realm, all people who reach maturity must pass through the stages of childhood, youth or adolescence, and adulthood. Spiritual development, although it may not happen at the same time, must pass through similar stages. From new birth and infancy, the Christian should progress through the trial and testing experiences of growing up until full Christian maturity is achieved. No matter what age a person is when he first accepts Jesus Christ as his Saviour, he must begin with the elementary truths and principles in his growth toward the perfect likeness of Christ.

Teach Children to Understand

The first stage in any learning experience is mental understanding. You need not understand all the theological principles of Scripture before you can experience salvation, but you must understand that all men are sinners, that Christ died for our sins, and that He will come into our lives if we invite Him. Without this simple understanding, the experience of salvation is impossible.

As you witness to any sinner, no matter what his age, you must begin with the first step, understanding. With the help of the Holy Spirit, this process of understanding can take place in an instant of supernatural enlightenment. Or, it may be the slower impartation of spiritual truth throughout childhood until the child finally comprehends the basic outline of God's plan of salvation. In either case, understanding precedes experience.

Make the Experience Relevant for Youth

Whereas children quite readily accept the explanations and instructions of parents and teachers, youth have reached the stage of questioning, of declaring their independence from tradition and accepted positions. Young people do not automatically subscribe to the views of their elders. Some, in fact, turn from those views and teachings just because they are held by their parents or teacher. It is at this stage of their lives that relevancy must be emphasized. A doctrine should be believed, not because adult theologians or scholars say it is true, but because God's Word declares it to be true and relevant to their daily activities and to their eternal destiny.

The best way to stress the relevancy of teaching is through demonstration, not by merely saying, "This truth is important to you." More than with any other age-level, the attitude of the teacher is important. The teacher is an authority figure, but youth are testing their personal relationship with all forms of authority—parental, educational, civil, and spiritual. The ingredient that makes the teacher's authority palatable to teenagers is an attitude of meekness.

Donald Gee makes this penetrating observation:

> We are to give an answer to those who ask us a reason of the hope that is in us "with meekness and fear" (1 Peter 3:15). The thought is that we are not to be unnecessarily argumentative and provocative in stating the grounds of our faith. Younger men, particularly, are prone to this fault. To win an argument can easily mean losing a soul. The *spirit* of our witness for Christ is the essence of its power. Men can feel our spirit even if our argument or testimony does not immediately convince them intellectually (*Fruitful or Barren* [Springfield, MO: Gospel Publishing House, 1961], p. 64).

Revitalize Old Truths for Adults

Some adults come into the Kingdom later in life. But like all Christians, their spiritual experience must progress through the stages of understanding, personal relevance, and vital experience. What a joy to see new converts, or newly baptized Christians, bubbling with the enthusiasm of a fresh experience.

But there are, unfortunately, more of the other kind of adult Christians—those whose experience of salvation and the baptism in the Holy Spirit took place years ago and for whom the memory is more vivid than the present reality. The truths have been heard, read, and recited so many times that they seem to have become commonplace and jaded. They no longer bring a tingle of joy and appreciation toward God for His grace and love. They no longer provide victorious confidence and sustaining strength for the routines of daily life.

Sad faces, fear, and timidity are quiet reminders that the vitality and forceful reality of doctrinal truth no longer motivates as it once did, or has not yet been appropriated at the level of victorious living that Scripture promises for the Christian.

These are the students that challenge the teacher of adults. The Holy Spirit must provide special anointing to keep the familiar truths of the everlasting gospel fresh and vibrant. When the cardinal doctrines, the foundations of our faith, are living realities in the lives of these students, the *go* of the Great Commission will reach into every neighborhood and work situation where revitalized Christians are found.

Understanding the Doctrine of Salvation

How can the teacher help children understand the basic truths of salvation? What are the basic principles of salvation that must be received by the understanding before the seed of faith can take root in the heart? What are the steps everyone must follow to receive the free salvation God has provided?

Salvation—More Than a Repair Kit

Some teachers and preachers place more emphasis on Satan than the enemy deserves. Even a child should understand that there is an adversary who tries to keep God's good from coming into our lives. But his work should never be portrayed in such a way that the child thinks more of Satan than he does of God and His love.

Be particularly careful in describing the entrance of sin into the world. Since the fall of Adam and Eve, the world has been under a curse; nature and our human existence are far less than they would be if Creation were today still in an unfallen state. But that does not mean that salvation is simply a repair kit to recover a little resemblance of the original perfection. Any work of God is of necessity perfect. And there are characteristics of the perfect work of salvation that surpass the innocent perfection of Creation. The relationship of the restored Christian to God is a tried and tested love exchange that has been refined by a knowledge and experience of sin and rebellion.

Memorize the following verses: Acts 16:31; Romans 3:23; 6:23.

Illustrations. Bring to class a magazine picture portraying a beautiful landscape or nature scene. Tear the picture in half in front of the class. Can that picture be restored to its original perfection? Cellophane tape will not do it. Even the most modern techniques of photograph restoration will leave some evidence of the tear. But God's salvation is more than a beautiful repair job. It is a new print, a new creation, with even more beauty added to the picture.

Sin Always Brings Ruin

No matter how attractive sin may appear—and having

one's selfish way seems attractive—sin always ends in ruin. *Illustrations* appropriate to the age-level are necessary to drive this point home.

Rodney always wanted to be first in everything. It was great fun. The first one to be the batter, or the first one to be the pitcher. The first to push his way onto the bicycle, the first to get the dessert at the dinner table. It always made him feel so important.

But things changed. The opportunities to be first became fewer and fewer. When he wanted to play ball, the others really didn't want to. Rod was still first, whenever he had a chance. But without any friends, there was no one to be second or third. It isn't as much fun to be first all alone. The sin of selfishness ruins friendships.

Jim and Timmy were told by Dad that they could use the lumber scraps from the new porch to build a playhouse in the backyard. After carrying everything around to the back, planning for the "second home" began. "Let's make it this way," suggested Jim, holding up two big boards.

"No, it will look better this way," Timmy said, as he grabbed the boards to show Jim what he wanted.

Boys will be boys, if Christ has not completed the transformation of their desires and actions. Soon the boards were weapons instead of rafters. The yelling and hatred were awful to see. Dad came running from the house to break up the fight—but not before the neighbors had opened their doors and windows to see what was happening. The Christian testimony of Jim and Timmy was ruined. Sin always ruins something.

The Steps of Salvation

God's part in our salvation is the most important part. But we also must do some things. The steps of salvation should be presented as follows:

1. *The Holy Spirit convicts of sin and makes man aware of his sinfulness.* "And when he [the Holy Spirit] has come he will convince the world of its sin, and of the availability of God's goodness, and of deliverance from judgment" (John 16:8, *The Living Bible).*

2. *The sinner admits that he is lost.* "No one is good—no one in all the world is innocent. No one has ever really followed God's paths, or even truly wanted to. Every one has turned away; all have gone wrong. No one anywhere has kept on doing what is right; not one" (Romans 3:10-12, *The Living Bible).*

3. *The sinner repents and asks for forgiveness.* Repentance means true sorrow for sin, with a sincere effort to forsake it. Repentance is shown in three ways: (1) confession of sin to God (Luke 18:13); (2) forsaking sin (Isaiah 55:7); and (3) turning to God (Acts 26:18).

4. *The sinner believes that Jesus died for him.* "Believe on the Lord Jesus Christ, and thou shalt be saved" (Acts 16:31).

5. *The sinner confesses Christ.* "For it is with your heart that you believe and are justified, and it is with your mouth that you confess and are saved" (Romans 10:10, *NIV).*

6. *The Holy Spirit makes the sinner a new person.* Christ now lives in the believer. "I have been crucified with Christ and I no longer live, but Christ lives in me. The life I live in the body, I live by faith in the Son of God, who loved me and gave himself for me" (Galatians 2:20, *NIV).*

7. *God justifies the believer.* "Through him everyone who believes is justified from everything from which you could not be justified by the law of Moses" (Acts 13:39, *NIV).*

8. *The one who once was lost has now been saved.*

Notice that man's part in salvation can be remembered

by the ABC of points 3, 4, and 5. After admitting that he is lost, man must *ask* for forgiveness, *believe* that Jesus died for him, and *confess* Christ. God does all the rest.

Making Salvation Relevant

Young people, especially teenagers, face a world quite different from that of their parents and other adults. Both age-groups, to be sure, read the same newspapers and have opportunity to view the same television programs. But the values and attitudes held by adults were formulated in a previous generation quite different from today's.

Some of the fault for the change must rest with the adult generation which has not vigorously opposed the new morality and values. Materialism rears its head in every conflict between management and labor. Humanism, or the elevation of man above God's Word or any system of absolutes, permeates our educational system and mass media. A worldly set of values and morality has replaced the ethical standards to which society seemed more committed in previous decades.

Adults with a vital Christian experience can shun these contemporary influences and live almost oblivious to their existence. But not so for the youth. The teacher of young people must be sensitive to the world his students face. He must encourage openness, accompanied by a spirit of meekness, as he leads teenagers and young adults to establish a value system and code of conduct based on God's Word. Important, therefore, are these vital truths of salvation.

Satan Is Real—And Seeking Your Ruin

Sin is not just a word for ignorance, sickness, or the absence of good. It represents rebellion against God, the breaking of divine principles that have been laid down for the good of all people. No matter how hard man works at domesticating and making sin look attractive, it still remains the ultimate enemy of man. And Satan, with whom all sin began, is more than a mythical figure dressed in a red suit complete with dart-shaped tail and horns. Satan is alive and making his presence felt wherever God is at work today.

Teenagers need constant reminders of the ugliness and final pain of sin. So many voices entice them with the external attractiveness of evil. Appropriate references in class to current newspaper accounts of personal disaster caused by sin will help develop an abhorrence of evil. Until young people hear the hiss of the serpent in sin, they will see it rather as doing one's own thing, as independence, or as exercising the rights of the individual. Salvation cannot become an inner reality until man realizes the sinfulness of his actions and desires victory over all sin.

Memorize the following verses: John 3:16; 2 Peter 3:9; 1 John 1:9; Revelation 3:20.

You Are Responsible and Must Give Account to God

One school of psychology sees man as an advanced animal. Like animals which act out of instinct and natural inclination, man only does what his natural inclinations lead him to do. Therefore, he cannot be held responsible for wrongdoing or sin, for his actions are the result of forces beyond his control. This view undermines the entire foundation of Christian faith, yet young people today are exposed to this philosophy of naturalism at school and in their interpersonal friendships. The theory of atheistic evolution describes man as the end result of impersonal and random genetic developments, no more than an animal without a soul or a moral conscience.

The absurdity of this position is easily demonstrated. If everyone really believed that man will never be called to give account for his choices and actions, anarchy would result. When every person looks out only for himself, the world becomes cruel and frightening. Yet that is the direction in which our world is moving today.

Salvation Is God's Work, but We Must Cooperate

At some time in their years of questioning and learning, young people and adults confront the problem of Calvinism and Arminianism. The difficulty is complicated by the fact that good evangelical Christians are divided on the question. But while Christians spend hours debating the question, Satan rejoices because witnessing and Christian service endeavors are diverted.

Don't contend for one extreme to the complete rejection of the other. There is truth to be defended in both positions, although the support of man's free will, along with an affirmation of God's sovereignty, will identify a person as Arminian (the customary classification of the Assemblies of God).

Illustration. D. L. Moody described the relation between God's sovereign election and man's free choice this way: "Election is a matter of God voting for you and the devil voting against you and whichever way you cast your vote that decides the matter." There may be a better theological explanation, but this does show the importance of man's choice.

God predestines "whosoever will" to be saved. Outside the door of salvation we read the words, "Whosoever will may come." After entering the door we read, "Elect according to the foreknowledge of God." God foreknows our destiny, but He does not determine it contrary to our free will.

Revitalizing the Doctrine of Salvation

Has the doctrine of salvation become commonplace to the longtime Christians of your acquaintance? Unfortunately, adults whose salvation experience lacks the initial vibrancy and joy are less than enthusiastic about sharing the experience with others, even their own children. The teacher of adults or young people who have grown up in Christian homes and accepted Christ at an early age must give continuous attention to keeping the reality of salvation alive and meaningful for his students.

This enthusiasm is demonstrated, not taught. It is imparted by Spirit-anointed teaching and by testimony from Christians whose salvation experience still pulsates with a vital relationship with Jesus Christ.

Regular reading of the Bible will keep the joy of salvation and the realization of what Christ has done for us from becoming a forgotten blessing. The scarlet thread of blood runs from Genesis to Revelation. God promised to send a Redeemer when He killed animals to make coats of skins for Adam and Eve. Abel killed a lamb to make an acceptable sacrifice. The Old Testament patriarchs built altars and made special sacrifices to Jehovah. During the last plague in Egypt, the visitation of the Death Angel, the blood sprinkled on the doorposts preserved the inhabitants within. The tabernacle in the wilderness and the many required sacrifices were shadows or types of the blood of Jesus which was to be shed for the sins of the world. The temple carried forward the same symbolism.

The focus of the Gospels—the ministry and death of Jesus—is the most brilliant appearance of the scarlet thread. And from the Last Supper until now, the Communion wine reminds us of the Blood atonement that has provided so many blessings for Christians today.

Memorize the following verses: John 4:14; Romans 5:1; Ephesians 2:8, 9; Hebrews 7:25.

Delivered From the Bondage of Sin

A chaplain walked up and down the aisle outside the death-row cells at the state penitentiary. Wherever possible, he stopped to share a witness for Christ. But in cell after cell, the response was the same, "The judge was unfair," "I didn't commit any crime," or, "The real criminal got off scot-free." Toward the end of the block was an inmate who sat on his cot with his head in his hands. In response to the chaplain's attempt to minister, a sob broke from the man's lips. "I've blown it; no one is to blame but myself. I feel rotten, miserable." The convict was the first convert in the chaplain's prison ministry.

Deliverance from sin can come only after one realizes that he is bound by sin. Then, no matter what happens to the outward man, it is the change that takes place within that counts. A Christian joined a crowd standing on a street corner listening to a soapbox orator extolling the virtues of socialism. "A new coat on every man in America" was his enthusiastic promise. Finally, the Christian could hold his silence no longer, "I know something better! Christ can put a new man in every coat in America!"

Paid in Full by Jesus Christ

Jesus cried from the cross, "It is finished." The word used for the expression in the original Greek really means, "It is done forever." The word was also used on tax receipts in ancient days and had the same meaning as the rubber-stamp message seen frequently today: "Paid in full." When Jesus uttered that triumphant word, our debt of sin was paid, completely satisfied. The atoning death of Jesus is the only basis on which sin can be forgiven.

The Assurance of Our Salvation

Martin Luther, the great Protestant reformer, recalled one of his battles with the devil.

"Do you feel like your sins are forgiven?" asked Satan.

"No, I don't feel that they are forgiven, but I know they are, because God says so in His Word!" Luther had an assurance of his salvation based on God's Word, not on his feelings.

Fanny Crosby had a vital and living salvation experience. Her songs reflect the joy and excitement of an intimate walk with Jesus. You may not have the talent to express your feelings the way she did, but you can sing the words she penned and feel the same exhilaration. If that foretaste of glory divine has grown bland, if the fact that you are His heir and purchase is just a line from a song, ask the Holy Spirit to make Jesus and His salvation real to you once again. Then you will sing with all the sincere conviction that stirs within: "Blessed assurance, Jesus is mine!"

4

The Promised Holy Spirit

Cardinal Doctrine Two

How many gods are there? Do we say with our mouths that there is only One, but then betray our real belief by speaking of and praying to three Persons—the Father, the Son, and the Holy Spirit?

There are some people—even evangelicals and Pentecostals—who do not believe in the Trinity. Unitarians deny the divinity of Jesus and say that God is a single Person. This doctrine is not Christian and is not difficult to disprove from the Bible. But what about those persons who do believe that Jesus Christ is divine but still refuse to believe that there are three Persons in the Godhead?

One group of people who hold this view are called the "Jesus Only" churches. They believe that the three Persons mentioned in the Bible are really only names for different manifestations of one Person. They speak of Jesus as the most important form of God because that is the form in which God revealed himself to man.

They further hold that before God appeared on earth in the form of Jesus, His name was the Father. But He stopped being the Father when He became the Son. Then when Jesus ascended into heaven and was no longer walking upon this earth, He took on the form of the Holy Spirit. So Jesus was in the form of the Father at one time, the human form of Jesus at another time, and finally in the form of the Holy Spirit at still another time. According to this heretical teaching, the three Persons have never existed at the same time. Can you refute this wrong belief from God's Word?

The Triune God

The best proof that there are three Persons in the Godhead—a Trinity—is the Gospel account of John's baptism of Jesus. You may study the story in Matthew 3:13-17, Mark 1:9-11, or Luke 3:21, 22. In this one incident, recorded in detail three times, we find all three members of the Trinity present at the same time: Jesus being baptized, the Holy Spirit descending like a dove, and the voice of the Father expressing approval from heaven. To explain this passage from a Jesus Only perspective, we would have to make Jesus a ventriloquist who bounced His words off the clouds: "This is my beloved Son, in whom I am well pleased."

What Is God Like?

When we speak of the attributes or characteristics of God, we are describing the qualities of each of the three Persons. When we find it necessary to note the unique characteristics of one of the three Persons, we must be careful to use the personal name.

It is true that the word *Trinity* does not appear in the New Testament. The word is a theological expression, first used during the second century, to describe a very obvious and frequently noted "threeness" within the unity of God. The divine unity is a multiple unity containing three distinct Persons, every One of whom is the Godhead, and yet each is supremely conscious of the other Two. The word *Trinity* is far different in meaning from *tritheism,* or the belief in three gods.

Since God is infinite in His being, it is impossible for any creature to know Him exactly as He is. So our answer to the question, "What is God like?" is destined to fall short of the full reality of this incomprehensible Being. Yet He has told us some things about himself that help us to understand in a limited way who He is and what He expects of us. The attributes of God indicate various sides of His character.

God Is a Spirit. He thinks, feels, speaks, and can have direct communion with His creatures made in His image. He cannot be seen with natural eyes or perceived by the natural senses. God can manifest himself in bodily form and thus be apprehended by man, but the essence of God cannot be seen (John 1:18; 4:24).

God Is Infinite. He is not subject to natural and human limitations. He is throughout, and greater than, His creation; and He is eternal (1 Kings 8:27; Revelation 4:8-10).

God Is Omnipotent. He is all-powerful (Job 42:2; Matthew 19:26; Revelation 19:6).

God Is Omnipresent. His presence is everywhere (Psalm 139:7-10; Jeremiah 23:23, 24).

God Is Omniscient. He knows all things. His knowledge is perfect; He does not have to reason, search, or learn gradually (Job 12:13; Job 36:4, 5; Proverbs 3:19).

God Is All-wise. In addition to knowing everything, God applies that knowledge in the best possible way to achieve the best possible purposes (Daniel 2:20-22; Ephesians 1:8).

God Is Sovereign. He has the absolute right to govern and deal with His creatures as He pleases (Daniel 4:35; Matthew 20:15; Romans 9:19-21).

God Is Holy. He is morally perfect, and He does only righteous acts (Isaiah 6:3; Genesis 18:25).

God Is Faithful. He is absolutely trustworthy; His

word will never fail (1 Corinthians 10:13; Matthew 24:35).

God Is Merciful. For one of the most eloquent reminders of the everlasting mercy of God, read Psalm 136. God's mercy was best manifested in sending Christ into the world (Luke 1:78).

God Is Love. This is the attribute of God that caused Him to send His Son to die for our sins (John 3:16).

God Is Good. God is so good in all His dealings with us (Psalms 34:8; 52:1).

What Is Distinctive About the Holy Spirit?

All of the things mentioned above about God are true of the Holy Spirit. But what can be said specifically about the person of the Holy Spirit?

The Holy Spirit is a Person because the Bible speaks of His mind (Romans 8:27), His will (1 Corinthians 12:11), and His feelings (Ephesians 4:30). These are all attributes of personality. Personal activities ascribed to Him include teaching (John 14:26), witnessing (Romans 8:16), speaking (Revelation 2:7), and revealing (2 Peter 1:21).

Some of the names by which the Holy Spirit is identified are helpful in calling attention to the distinctive characteristics of the Third Person of the Trinity. As the *Spirit of God,* He is an executive carrying out the will of God. As the *Spirit of Christ* (Romans 8:9), He comes in the name of Christ and gives glory to the Son. As the *Comforter* or *Paraclete* (John 14:16), He stands beside and sustains believers in their time of need. As the *Holy Spirit,* He seeks to impart holiness and sanctification to us.

As the *Holy Spirit of Promise* (Ephesians 1:13), He is the manifestation of God that was promised throughout the Old Testament. As the *Spirit of Truth* (John 14:17),

His mission is to reveal Jesus Christ, the Way, the Truth, and the Life. As the *Spirit of Grace* (Hebrews 10:29), He imparts grace and power for living a sanctified life. As the *Spirit of Life* (Romans 8:2), He gives and preserves both natural and spiritual life. As the *Spirit of Adoption* (Romans 8:15), He brings us into the family of God.

Sanctification Through the Spirit

Instantaneous Sanctification

For most people, salvation is an experience that can be pinpointed as to place and time. For others, the experience took place at such an early age that no first time or place can be identified. In either case, however, there was a work of the Holy Spirit that brought the believer into the family of God. But there is a work of sanctification that takes place beyond salvation.

Progressive Sanctification

We should not remain in the same condition in which we find ourselves immediately after conversion. Christ expects us to become more and more like Him. This process by which we become more like Him is called "progressive sanctification"; it is distinct from positional or instantaneous sanctification that takes place at the moment of salvation.

As we daily become more like Jesus, there are four things that happen in our lives. First, we more completely present our lives to God. "I beseech you therefore, brethren, by the mercies of God, that ye present your bodies a living sacrifice, holy, acceptable unto God, which is your reasonable service" (Romans 12:1).

Second, there is growth from spiritual infancy toward spiritually mature Christianity (1 Corinthians 3:1; 2 Peter

3:18). Third, we are continually cleansed and purified from all filthiness of the flesh and the spirit (2 Corinthians 7:1). Finally, we are transformed, day by day, into a more Christlike person. The Holy Spirit is the primary Agent in bringing about these changes in our lives.

The Baptism in the Holy Spirit

The Holy Spirit works in the lives of all believers after conversion to make them more like Jesus. But there is an experience that holds the potential for accelerating the process of making us more Christlike. It is described in Acts 2 and is the distinctive belief of all Christians who call themselves Pentecostals.

The Experience and Its Initial Evidence

Jesus first gave promise of the experience as He was about to leave His disciples: "It is expedient for you that I go away: for if I go not away, the Comforter will not come unto you; but if I depart, I will send him unto you. . . . When he, the Spirit of truth, is come, he will guide you into all truth" (John 16:7, 13). He reaffirmed the promise after His resurrection and just before He ascended into heaven: "But ye shall receive power, after that the Holy Ghost is come upon you: and ye shall be witnesses unto me . . ." (Acts 1:8).

Then it happened! The sound of wind, the cloven tongues of fire, the speaking in tongues! The promise had been fulfilled—or so it has been thought by some. "No," said Peter, "this is just a beginning." "For the promise is unto you, and to your children, and to all that are afar off, even as many as the Lord our God shall call" (Acts 2:39).

How is the experience received? In much the same way that salvation was received earlier. A right attitude is essential. The group on whom the Spirit was first out-poured knew unity and prayed in one accord. Obedience to God is necessary, because "God hath given [the Holy Spirit] to them that obey him" (Acts 5:32). Just as faith is required in salvation, so we must have faith to receive this gift of power and consecration.

How do we know when a person receives the charismatic impartation of the Holy Spirit? This question has caused much controversy and has been a major point of disagreement between Pentecostals and non-Pentecostal evangelicals. The Pentecostal position that speaking in tongues is the initial physical evidence of the baptism in the Holy Spirit is based on the five instances of such infillings recorded in the Book of Acts (chapters 2, 8, 9, 10, 19).

In three of the five records, the believers all spoke in Spirit-given languages upon receiving the Baptism. In the other two instances, the speaking in other tongues is implied: Simon the Sorcerer desired to buy the gift because of some obvious external manifestation (Acts 8), and Paul had the manifestation at some time because he later testified that he spoke in tongues more than the believers to whom he wrote (Acts 9; 1 Corinthians 14:18). The Holy Spirit dwells in every believer, but every believer has not been baptized in the Holy Spirit.

Continuing Evidence of a Spirit-filled Life

An initial infilling, accompanied by speaking in tongues, is not intended by God to be the extent of one's walk with the Spirit. There are two important aspects to our life in the Spirit: (1) receiving the Baptism initially and (2) remaining filled with the Spirit as a vital power and presence in our lives.

What is the evidence that a Christian is currently filled with and completely controlled by the Holy Spirit? What are the marks of the truly spiritual person? Paul reminds us in 1 Corinthians 13 that we can speak with tongues, possess the gift of prophecy, understand all mysteries and knowledge, and have faith that moves mountains—and still be nothing! A great big *zero* in God's sight. The real test is the love which must motivate the gifts.

Jesus said it another way: "By their fruits ye shall know them. . . . Many will say to me in that day, Lord, Lord, have we not prophesied in thy name? and in thy name have cast out devils? and in thy name done many wonderful works? And then will I profess unto them, I never knew you: depart from me" (Matthew 7:20, 22). So the fruit—more specifically the fruit of the Spirit—gives evidence that the Holy Spirit continues to dwell within us in His fullness.

Love. Some scholars indicate that Galatians 5:22, 23 can be translated as follows: "But the fruit of the Spirit is love: that is, joy, peace, long-suffering, kindness, goodness, faithfulness, meekness, self-control." If you really have *divine* love, that will take care of all the details. You can check yourself to see if you have it by asking if you have joy, peace, patience, kindness, and all the rest, including meekness and self-control.

Joy. The joy of the Spirit is much more than natural joy. It exists even in the midst of sorrow and disappointment. In fact, it is birthed in suffering. Jesus himself said that divine joy works that way (John 16:20, 21).

Peace. The peace the Spirit gives is the same kind of peace Jesus promised His disciples: "My peace I give unto you: not as the world giveth, give I unto you. Let not your heart be troubled, neither let it be afraid" (John 14:27).

Patience. "Lord, make me patient—NOW." But it doesn't happen that way. Tribulation develops patience through the work of the Holy Spirit.

Kindness. This fruit is related to mercy and grace—unmerited or undeserved kindness. The Spirit wants to develop this Godlike fruit in us.

Goodness. In a world that epitomizes just the opposite, the Spirit desires to produce integrity, morality, and deeds of goodness and generosity.

Faithfulness. Christ is our faithful High Priest, and notice what compassion and sacrifice He demonstrated. The Spirit seeks to develop the same fruit in us.

Meekness. Like the related fruit of gentleness or kindness, this fruit is humanly impossible to achieve. But the meek shall inherit the earth (Matthew 5:5).

Self-control. This fruit regulates and binds together all the other fruit. Love without restraint becomes passion. Joy without moderation becomes frivolity. Peace without temperance becomes idleness. Patience without balance is apathy. Gentleness without temperance is weakness. Goodness without control becomes fawning. Faith without moderation of reason becomes blind superstition. And meekness without temperance is timidity.

The Spirit seeks to produce all these fruit in the life of Spirit-filled Christians. Some are quick to argue, however, "I know many non-Pentecostals who demonstrate more fruit of the Spirit than do those who claim to be filled with the Spirit."

This observation, though, does not destroy the validity of the Spirit's work. He works faithfully with the raw material that is surrendered to Him. How much less admirable would be the Pentecostal without the work of the Spirit; and how much more pleasing to God would be the one who has produced some good natural fruit, if he received the full work of the Spirit. For whatever good there is in us, we must give the credit to God. And the Spirit has an even greater work to do in each of us.

Sins Against the Spirit

The work of the Spirit in individual lives can bring great blessing. But there are corresponding responsibilities expected of each person in whom the Spirit moves. We must cooperate with the work that the Spirit seeks to accomplish. The Bible lists several ways in which Christians can hinder the move of the Spirit. We can lie to Him (Acts 5:3, 4), grieve Him (Ephesians 4:30), quench His power (1 Thessalonians 5:19), resist Him (Acts 7:51), or blaspheme His person (Matthew 12:31, 32). The latter two sins seem to describe potential actions of unbelievers or apostates. Christians grieve the Spirit when they fail to use the provision of the indwelling Holy Spirit to produce holy and fruitful lives. They quench the Spirit when they do not allow Him to endue them with power and use them in His service.

The Gifts and Ministries of the Holy Spirit

1 Corinthians 12:8-10	*1 Corinthians 12:28-30*	*Romans 12:4-8*	*Ephesians 4:11*
	Apostles		Apostles
			Evangelists
	Teachers	Teaching	Pastor-teachers
Word of Wisdom			
Word of Knowledge			
Faith			
Gifts of Healing	Gifts of Healings		
Working of Miracles	Workers of Miracles		
Prophecy	Prophets	Prophecy	Prophets
Discerning of Spirits			
Divers Kinds of Tongues	Diversities of Tongues		
Interpretation of Tongues	Interpretation of Tongues		
	Helps	Ministry (Service)	
	Governments	Ruling	
		Exhortation	
		Giving	
		Showing Mercy	

The Gifts and Special Ministries of the Spirit

Some people speak of the nine fruit of the Spirit (Galatians 5:22, 23) and the nine gifts of the Spirit (1 Corinthians 12:8-10) as though these two lists contained a total description of the ministry of the Spirit. But there are other passages that must be considered: 1 Corinthians 12:28-30; Romans 12:4-8; and Ephesians 4:11. Since there is obvious repetition or overlapping in the lists, they are summarized in the accompanying chart. Notice that *prophecy* or *prophets* is mentioned in all four lists, *teachers* or *teaching* in three lists, and *apostles, healings, miracles, tongues, interpretation, helps* (service), and *administration* are mentioned in two lists. So the ministries of the Holy Spirit are extremely many and varied.

The Gifts of the Spirit

Although the four lists are interrelated, there is also an obvious difference between the treatment of the list in 1 Corinthians 12:8-10 and the other lists.

As the situation demands or the need arises, the Spirit can touch one believer or another to accomplish His work in edifying the entire Body. The various gifts are not given as permanent possessions of the recipient to be used arbitrarily as he or she desires. The Spirit may at any time choose a new channel for His operation of bringing edification to the Body.

The Word of Wisdom. The supernatural inspiration for speaking the right word at the right time. The "word of wisdom" is literally the "utterance of divine wisdom." "If any of you lack wisdom, let him ask of God, that giveth to all men liberally" (James 1:5).

The Word of Knowledge. The supernaturally inspired utterance of facts that could only be known by God and revealed to the believer by the Holy Spirit. The word of knowledge suggests insight into divine things, while the word of wisdom is the ability to use knowledge in a prudent manner.

Faith. A special impartation of faith to meet an emergency or a critical circumstance with the assurance that miraculous intervention will follow.

Gifts of Healing. A special enduement of power which results in the healing of disease, illness, or physical infirmity.

Working of Miracles. Works of divine power, other than healing, that demonstrate God's intervention in the natural order of things.

Prophecy. The utterance of a divine truth in a person's own language, as prompted by the Holy Spirit. Since this gift lacks the supernatural physical evidence that characterizes the other gifts, an additional word of caution is in order. Because we are not always as closely aligned with God as we should be, we as believers face the danger of making ourselves independent of God's leading by speaking our own words and acting in our own power—but still implying that we are speaking and acting for God.

Peter's admonition is important: "Each one should use whatever spiritual gift he has received to serve others, faithfully administering God's grace in its various forms. If anyone speaks, he should do it as one speaking the very words of God. If anyone serves, he should do it with the strength God provides, so that in all things God may be praised through Jesus Christ" (1 Peter 4:10, 11, *NIV).*

"As one speaking the very words of God" does not mean that we should speak like a prophet even when the words and ideas are our own. It means rather that we should always permit God to speak through us and demonstrate His power through our service. Only then will edification result.

Discerning of Spirits. The God-given discernment to

detect the difference between words or acts inspired by God, by Satan, and by the human spirit. Through this gift, one may also discern a person's spiritual character. Care must be taken to distinguish this gift from natural insight into human nature or from a fault-finding spirit.

Divers Kinds of Tongues. The power of speaking supernaturally in a language never learned by the speaker. Tongues delivered as a definite message for the church, or to lead in public worship, must be followed by the supernatural gift of interpretation. This manifestation of tongues should be distinguished from tongues as the initial evidence of the Baptism and tongues as ecstatic praise or intercessory prayer addressed to God alone.

Interpretation of Tongues. Just as the utterance in tongues is not conceived in the human mind, so the interpretation emanates from the Spirit rather than from the intellect. Tongues plus interpretation are equal to prophecy (1 Corinthians 14:5). Tongues, however, may serve as a sign for the unbeliever (v. 22).

Regulation of the Gifts in Public Worship. The manifestations of the Spirit must be regulated according to God-ordained controls so they edify the body of Christ. First Corinthians 14 contains guidelines to assure that the gifts accomplish God's purpose for which they are given. The highlights of the regulations are: (1) All things should be done decently and in order and (2) for edification (1 Corinthians 14:26, 40). Other recommendations in the exercise of the individual gifts are balance of emphasis (vv. 12-15), use of common sense or mature understanding (v. 20), self-control by the believer (v. 32), and cultivation of humility and a teachable spirit (v. 37).

Offices and Ministries Energized by the Spirit

As we study Ephesians 4:11, 1 Corinthians 12:28-30,

and Romans 12:4-8, we become aware of a shift in emphasis from the gifts to specialized ministries that Spirit-filled believers have been given. As one of the gifts is seen to operate with greater regularity in one believer than in others, we conclude that the words of 1 Corinthians 12:28 are being fulfilled: "God hath set some in the church" for special offices or ministries. These are therefore Spirit-appointed and anointed functions or offices that constitute specialized callings or ministries. No believer, however, can expect an exclusive ministry, for the Spirit may choose to anoint others for a similar ministry.

Drawing from the chart on the gifts and ministries of the Holy Spirit, we recognize the following offices that are specially used by God to bring edification to His children. Some of the ministries may seem to be natural human abilities, but in each case the Holy Spirit is working in and through, and going beyond, the believer's natural ability for the common good of the people of God.

Apostle. A person specially sent by God to open new fields and churches, to lay the foundation on which others will build. Paul is the best example.

Prophet. A person specially commissioned to speak the things of God and His righteousness. Sometimes he must denounce sin in high places, as John the Baptist did in the presence of Herod.

Evangelist. A person who has a special calling to bring the gospel to everyone possible. Like Philip, he sows the seed and then moves on to sow the seed elsewhere. Other ministries must cooperate to conserve the new harvest.

Pastor. A person called to care for and feed the sheep; a shepherd to the flock.

Teacher. A person called to lead people, through instruction, into the path of full discipleship.

Helps or Ministry. Any form of Christian service that

contributes to the good of the Christian body. An usher or a Sunday school secretary may perform Spirit-anointed tasks that make the ministry of the church more effective.

Governments, Ruling, or Administration. For the most efficient operation of the church, there must be Spirit-directed leadership.

Exhortation. The supernatural ministry of challenging the sinner and the saint to turn from wrong to right, from error to truth, from rebellion to obedience and faith.

Giving or Christian Benevolence. The Holy Spirit anoints some believers to a practical manifestation of love and unselfishness.

Showing Mercy. This office seems vacant too frequently, but the Spirit desires to call believers to demonstrate special sympathy and understanding.

Led and Empowered by the Spirit

The life or walk in the Spirit is exciting! Each day is a new experience. We find ourselves saying, "What beautiful work of the Spirit will I see or be a part of today?"

Guidance

"When he, the Spirit of truth, is come, he will guide you into all truth" (John 16:13). This guidance comes mainly through the illumination of the Word of God. But the Holy Spirit is faithful to guide us in matters that are not within the direct application of Scripture. As the mind of Christ dwells within us, we can prayerfully and confidently make decisions and take steps of faith through the quiet prompting of the Holy Spirit. If our hearts are sensitive to the gentle checks of the Spirit or genuinely thankful for closed doors, we can move through the Christian walk with the assurance that the Spirit's guidance is always there when we need it.

Witnessing and Service

"Ye shall receive power, after that the Holy Ghost is come upon you: and ye shall be witnesses unto me" (Acts 1:8). If our witnessing and service are to be powerful and effective, we must continually be anointed by the Holy Spirit. The offices and ministries studied earlier in this chapter are not just occupations or specialized human abilities. The Spirit who sets believers apart for such tasks also gives the power to perform them successfully.

The Holy Spirit is more than a cardinal doctrine. He is a Person who desires to be the energizing and fulfilling Force in our lives. We today can experience the guidance and power for witnessing as Philip did. "The Spirit told Philip, 'Go to that chariot and stay near it' " (Acts 8:29, *NIV*). The power of Philip's witness led to the conversion of the Ethiopian eunuch and an effective witness in northeast Africa.

5

Teaching Students About the Holy Spirit

Cardinal Doctrine Two

The world is facing a crisis of fairly recent origin—the energy crisis. For years it was thought that the vast underground supplies of natural gas and oil were inexhaustible. A few voices gave warning of an approaching shortage, but people living in affluence found the caution hard to believe.

Suddenly we find ourselves with insufficient supplies to heat and power our growing housing and industrial facilities. The price of driving our automobiles has increased alarmingly. Devastating inflation affects everyone. At first, we suspected conspiracy and the manipulation of prices and supplies. But now the world is scrambling to find alternatives. Countries without sufficient supplies of their own court the favor of the oil-rich nations in a struggle to preserve their own economy.

But there is another energy crisis—a spiritual energy crisis. This one is quite different. The supply is unlimited, yet the majority of people fail to draw on the energy source. The problem is a long-standing one—existing for as long as man has been under the curse of sin.

The Bible tells us of the supernatural power and energizing strength available to Christians through the work of the Holy Spirit. But sinners refuse to allow the Spirit to do His work in their lives, and Christians live below the provision of supernatural power that has been made available to them. People search for alternative sources of spiritual power and energy—the power of the mind, of non-Christian religions, and even of satanically inspired spirits. Yet the true supply is unlimited; it need only be allowed to work in individual lives.

Understanding the Doctrine of the Holy Spirit

When children or new Christians are first introduced to the concept of the Holy Spirit, there is frequently a hesitation or skepticism. The way in which such a person first conceives of the doctrine of the Holy Spirit is very important. Some people have had a lifelong bias against the Pentecostal experience because some well-meaning but uninformed opponent of the experience described all kinds of bizarre myths and half-truths about Spirit-filled Christians.

Memorize the following verses: John 4:24; Acts 1:8; Ephesians 5:18.

Explaining the Person of the Holy Spirit

The concept of the Trinity causes some children and adults difficulty when it is first presented. There is only one true God, yet there are three Persons in the Godhead: Father, Son, and Holy Spirit. To some this seems like a contradiction, and they have been swept into non-Trinitarian groups like "Jesus Only." So instruction concerning the truth of the Trinity is very important.

Use as many of the following illustrations for the Trinity as are appropriate for the age-level you are teaching.

Water. The one element at different temperatures can be vapor (steam or fog), liquid, or ice (snow).

Electricity. Depending on the appliance into which the electricity flows, it can become light, heat, or power (in machines).

Three-leafed shamrock or clover. All three parts are needed to have one complete leaf.

One light from three candles. Light three candles in a dark room, but there is only one light, not three.

Triangle. This geometric figure has three sides, or three angles, but it is still one triangle.

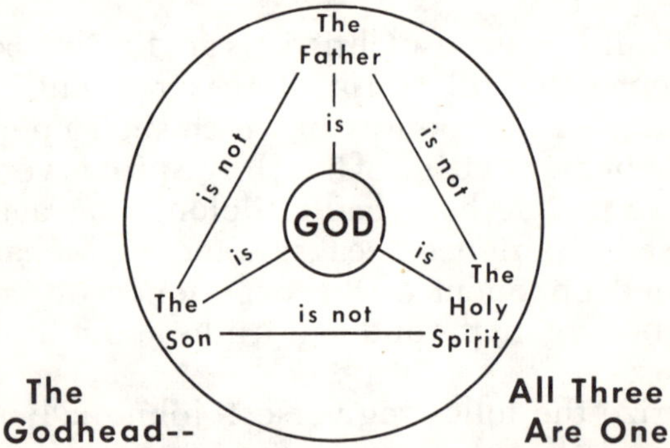

The following triangle can be cut from lightweight cardboard and rotated on a pin inserted in the center, while Luke 3:22 is recited and discussed by the class.

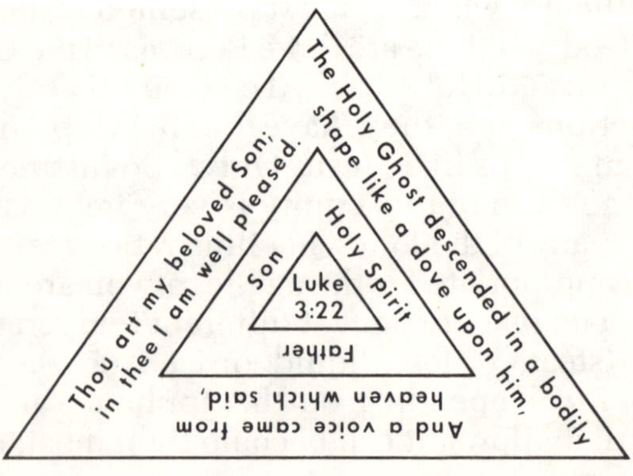

Overcoming Fear of the Holy Ghost

The translators of the King James Version did not intend that readers should think of the Holy Spirit as a disembodied ghost. In the 16th century, the words *ghost* and *spirit* meant the same thing. Children think of ghosts as disembodied spirits of dead persons that appear to living persons as pale, shadowy apparitions. This may hinder their complete submission to the working of the Holy Spirit.

A good way of overcoming any fear that children might have of the Holy Spirit and of His manifestations is to describe Him as a close Friend. Solomon refers to "a friend that sticketh closer than a brother" (Proverbs 18:24). The Holy Spirit certainly fits this description.

The story of Elijah's translation (2 Kings 2) will help children understand that the anointing of the Spirit is the act of a Friend, not a mysterious force that moves people against their will. Dramatize the friendship between Elijah and Elisha as seen in Elisha's determination not to leave Elijah. For his devotion to his earthly friend, the divine Friend of Elijah became Elisha's Friend in double portion. Elisha wanted a closer friendship and enduement of the Spirit that had been closer to Elijah than a brother.

Explaining the Power of the Holy Spirit

Children should not be afraid of the manifestations of the Spirit. A loving and warm attitude toward the subject will help set the proper tone. Comparing the power of the Holy Spirit to electricity may be of value.

Bring a small table lamp to class (if your students are juniors or older). With the bulb inserted properly, ask a student to turn on the lamp. Unscrew the bulb from the socket. Be careful that no child comes near the lamp during this phase of the discussion. Ask if anyone is willing to put a finger in the open socket. If someone is, you will need to discuss briefly the dangers of improperly controlled electricity. Also, without a bulb inserted in the socket, the lamp could sit on the table forever and never give proof of the power supply to which it is connected.

The Holy Spirit is a Friend who gives us power to live pure lives and shine as witnesses in a dark world.

Making the Holy Spirit Relevant

The Holy Spirit wants to be an indwelling Friend of adults, youth, and children. Children should be encouraged to open their hearts to the baptism in the Holy Spirit. Sometimes, however, the understanding or readiness comes with growing mental and emotional maturity. But by the time a young person becomes a teenager, he or she needs the experience of Pentecost as an undergirding for the problems faced in the adolescent world.

When was the last time you impressed on the members of your teenage class their need of being filled with the Holy Spirit?

Some teachers may feel that urging young people to seek for the Baptism should be left to the pastor or evangelist. But in neglecting to stress the Baptism we are depriving our teenagers of the very experience they need for meeting the many problems of growth and maturation.

The teenager lives in a world of confusion. His reaction to this confusion is *indecision.* Is it any wonder that he is often unpredictable—that he reacts first in one way to a particular situation and then a short time later in an opposite fashion? The only answer to this boiling indecision is the guiding presence of the Holy Spirit. This Comforter will help him with his daily living. Even teenagers who have been reared in Pentecostal homes need teaching on the baptism in the Holy Spirit, for Christian parents sometimes take the spiritual understanding of their children for granted.

Memorize the following verses: Joel 2:28; Acts 2:4; Galatians 5:22, 23, 25.

Teaching Teens About the Spirit-controlled Life

Sanctification and separation from the world seem to be foreign concepts for many young people. The emphasis rather is on asking, "What is wrong with. . . ?" or, "Why can't I do it? Everyone else is." These questions must be given loving and meek answers, but leading teenagers into the Spirit-controlled life will supply more meaningful answers.

There is far more to the Spirit-filled life than "can'ts" and "don'ts." For everything we are separated from, as the Spirit controls our lives, there is something better in its place.

Teens need to be taught the joy of walking in the Spirit, of manifesting the fruit of the Spirit in their daily lives. At first glance, teenagers find little attraction in such virtues as patience, gentleness, and meekness. But the Holy Spirit transforms what seems like weakness into supernatural strength. There is power in these fruit.

Most Christians are unwilling to admit weakness or to become vulnerable in front of others. They fear that they will lose too much. But the truth is just the opposite. We lose more by not following Christ's pattern. The Beatitudes of Matthew 5 tell us the rewards of each Spirit-produced fruit:

The meek shall inherit the earth.

The gentle or merciful shall receive mercy.

The patient in persecution shall receive heaven.

Earth, heaven, and God's mercy are unbeatable rewards for allowing the Holy Spirit to develop the fruit of meekness, gentleness, and patience in our lives.

The Spirit and the Success Syndrome

There are people today who claim that financial success is the mark of God's blessing, that God intended His children to be affluent and comfortable, not poor or limited. This misleading explanation of God's blessing in terms of financial resources is dangerous for youth as well as for adults. But there is a sense in which the indwelling presence of the Holy Spirit is the greatest guarantee of success a person can have.

Teenagers have goals, ambitions, and plans. They should be taught that these are within reach if they are in line with Biblical principles and standards. The Spirit is a Counselor who will guide us in making decisions concerning our entire future. The outpouring of the Spirit today among laymen in various professions is a fulfillment of the promise that the Spirit would be poured out on all flesh. Even the professional sports—football, baseball, basketball—have dedicated Spirit-filled Christians who are taking the gospel witness to these areas and to the youth whom athletes influence so strongly.

God wants His children to succeed in any area to which He has called them. And He seems to be calling them into positions that were once thought to be void of a Christian witness. In working with teenagers, take advantage whenever possible of the many testimonies of major public figures who have committed their entire lives to a witness for Christ.

Revitalizing the Doctrine of the Holy Spirit

It seems unbelievable that a dynamic experience like the baptism in the Holy Spirit and the exciting walk that follows would ever lose their vitality. But for many who sit in the pews of our churches, they have. One reason is that the initial experience has been emphasized so strongly that the continuing life in the Spirit is overlooked or neglected.

There is more to the Pentecostal experience than speaking in tongues at an altar after a soul-stirring sermon. For those who have progressed no further in their spiritual experience, or who have allowed the original fervor to cool to a lukewarm apathy, the doctrine of the Holy Spirit needs to be revitalized.

Immersion in New Testament Pentecost

Every Pentecostal Christian should read the Book of Acts at least once a year. The excitement and vitality of Early Church Pentecost is the best encouragement to a Pentecostal testimony and demonstration today. All five instances of infilling by the Holy Spirit (Acts 2; 8; 9; 10; and 19) should be studied in depth in various translations.

The people who made up the Early Church were people just like Christians today. They had similar desires, struggles with the flesh, and needs for divine help in their daily lives. Don't place the New Testament saints on a pedestal high above the plane of ordinary people. Identify with them as you read the historical accounts of the Spirit's work among these early believers. Encourage your students to become similarly involved in the Pentecostal experiences recorded in the New Testament.

Memorize the following verses: John 14:16; 16:13; Romans 8:26; 1 Corinthians 12:4-6.

The Offices of the Spirit

The Scriptures use a variety of names for the person and work of the Holy Spirit. John 14 through 17 should be studied carefully. The Holy Spirit is our Comforter, Teacher, Counselor, and Adviser. In the Book of Romans we see Him as our Intercessor. He is also our Standby and Strengthener.

These descriptive names for the Holy Spirit are especially meaningful for adults and should be stressed in personalizing the ministry of the Holy Spirit in their lives. In the middle-age years, adults face important decisions concerning employment, family, and future security. Senior citizens find themselves facing problems of loneliness, isolation, insecurity, and dwindling resources. The Holy Spirit is the Friend, Comforter, and Strengthener these adults need. Lead them to know this special Person of the Godhead more intimately.

Enduement for Service

A real mark of spiritual maturity is the move from self-centered concern ("What can the Holy Spirit do in my life and for my needs?") to concern for ministry to others ("What can the Holy Spirit do through me to meet the needs of others around me?"). We need to spend more time learning and practicing the concepts of 1 Corinthians 12 and 14, tempered by the love emphasis of chapter 13.

The gifts of the Spirit are given for the edification of the body of Christ. Every Spirit-filled believer is a member of Christ's body and should make definite contributions, prompted by the Holy Spirit, to the spiritual growth of others.

Wherever you find your students in their spiritual development, lead them on through understanding to full appropriation of all the Holy Spirit wants to do in the life of every Christian. Let them know, "This Baptism is for you."

6

The Provision of Divine Healing

Cardinal Doctrine Three

The doctrine of divine healing has held more problems for Pentecostal Christians than any of the other three cardinal doctrines. There is no difficulty in reading and understanding what seems to be the message of Scripture on the subject. But problems arise when reality—what we observe in the lives of Christians—is set over against the positive statements of God's Word.

Attempts have been made to resolve the conflict between the emphatic promises concerning divine healing and the obvious lack of consistent healings and universal health among Christians by blaming the sick for their lack of faith, by reinterpreting Scripture to conform to "the real-life situation," or by denying the reality of sickness through positive thinking or other mind-over-body techniques.

We live in an age of unbelief—even in churches. The preacher and teacher spend more time explaining why many are not healed than they spend in encouragement or the building of faith. And when the messenger boldly proclaims the message of deliverance and healing, the listeners allow thoughts of doubt to bind the potential power that God desires to be released in every congregation. "But Sister Jones seems so dedicated, and yet she isn't healed." "If divine healing really works, why hasn't someone traveled the corridors of the hospitals and sent the sick and the injured home with a new vigor and life?" "Is he really preaching all the truth about divine healing, or just the positive side?"

You have heard the questions, or maybe even thought them yourself. God invites questions from the honest inquirer, especially from the young Christian who lacks a deeper understanding of the Word. This may explain why some of "the least worthy" or most unlikely persons receive healing while the churches have sickly saints who can claim God's promise of grace in suffering but never enter into a complete deliverance.

God seems to expect more from mature Christians, both the sick and the healthy. There is a fine line between sincere questioning and doubt. This fact seems to be the point of James 1:6: "Ask in faith, nothing wavering: for he that wavereth is like a wave of the sea driven with the wind and tossed." And again: "Let us hold fast the profession of our faith without wavering" (Hebrews 10:23). When our questioning reveals a wavering faith, the flow of the Holy Spirit in healing is greatly hindered.

Our study of divine healing will recognize that there are times when healing does not come—at least in the manner and at the time we have requested. But let that matter rest until later. Open your heart to the truth of God's Word on divine healing without the wavering of questions at this point.

The Source of Sickness and Death

Sickness and sin are related, but not in a way that permits us to blame every sickness on sin in the life of the sufferer. Health, rather than sickness, was God's original intention for the human race. But the first act of disobedience in the Garden of Eden brought sickness on Adam and Eve and all their descendents. "By man came death [and sickness], . . . in Adam all die" (1 Corinthians 15:21, 22). Our participation in Adam's sin is verified every time we are disobedient. Both sickness and death are consequences of the Fall, so man's sin explains why sickness is a fact of life.

Satan as the Agent of Sickness

Since sickness is a manifestation of sin in the world, God does not cause sickness. On the other hand, sickness is not an evidence that Satan has overcome God and His ability to create and recreate health and wholeness. Just as God has allowed Satan a limited dominion over the world as a direct consequence of the Fall, so He has permitted Satan a limited power to use sickness as a part of his evil influence in the world.

Since sickness originates in sin and the work of Satan, it represents a challenge to God's sovereignty; this challenge, though, was answered by Jesus Christ in His healing ministry while He was on earth and through His healing touch still today. Satan is working in some fashion in sickness, for he delights in causing physical suffering and pain.

God is sovereign in all human affairs and particularly so in the lives of believers. We must therefore conclude that sickness can touch the believer only as God permits it. Yet God is not responsible for illness and suffering because He has divine purposes to accomplish when He allows Satan, through sickness, to afflict the believer temporarily. God works in the lives of believers by turning sickness into an agent for spiritual growth and by demonstrating that He has triumphed over the curse Satan has brought on the human race.

The Functions of Sickness in the Believer

Although Satan is the agent of sickness, God is still in control and accomplishes His purposes through the experience. Sickness can serve as *a teacher* in the learning of some spiritual truths. Paul's thorn in the flesh (2 Corinthians 12:7) served to remind him of the sufficient grace and strength of Jesus Christ. Sickness can also perform the task of *a disciplinarian* to correct or call back from a wrong pathway. Miriam was temporarily smitten with leprosy (Numbers 12:10) for her murmuring against Moses.

Sickness can function as *a judge* who pronounces a penalty for sin or wrongdoing. King Jehoram (2 Chronicles 21:18, 19) was stricken by an incurable disease because of his wicked life and his failure to repent even after the beginning of the sickness. Sickness can serve as an *example* to others of some truth that God desires to illustrate. As in the case of Job, this type of suffering should end when God's purpose is accomplished.

Limits to the Work of Satan

If death is not evidence of Satan's victory, then neither is sickness. "Death is swallowed up in victory. . . . Thanks be to God, which giveth us the victory through our Lord Jesus Christ" (1 Corinthians 15:54, 57). Believers can have the victory even while they wait for healing. Satan has been defeated, the price has been paid. We wait only for the outward evidence of that already accomplished victory—in the lives of believers now and throughout all creation at the Great Restoration Day.

Healing is definitely for *now*. Each triumph of restored health is another evidence that God has overcome the rebellion and evil of Satan, even though He has not yet finally disposed of all sickness and death. But that promise will be fulfilled as certainly as Christ came to earth to die for our sins. "And God shall wipe away all tears from their eyes; and there shall be no more death, neither sorrow, nor crying, neither shall there be any more pain: for the former things are passed away" (Revelation 21:4).

The Promise of Health and Healing

God has always been a God who heals. To the Israelites He said, "I am the Lord that healeth thee" (Exodus 15:26). On another occasion He promised as a reward for obedience, "The Lord will take away from thee all sickness, and will put none of the evil diseases of Egypt . . . upon thee" (Deuteronomy 7:15).

But the greatest proof that God is by nature a Healer comes in Jesus Christ, the incarnate form of Deity. Isaiah prophesied that the Messiah would heal the sick: "With his stripes we are healed" (Isaiah 53:5). "The Spirit of the Lord God is upon me; because the Lord hath anointed me to preach good tidings unto the meek; he hath sent me to bind up the brokenhearted" (Isaiah 61:1). Healing is a part of God's very nature.

The Purpose of Healing

Healing or health is not an end in itself. To ask for healing merely to escape pain or suffering may reveal a self-centered or selfish motivation. The same principle is true, of course, in all areas of our lives. Why do we desire success, material comforts, or security? God sometimes knows our hearts better than we do. Could it be that He withholds some of our desires in order to turn us, in our restlessness and weakness, to Him and to His strength and complete sufficiency? The divine admonition of Jesus no doubt applies to physical healing as well as to material blessings: "But seek ye first the kingdom of God, and his righteousness; and all these things shall be added unto you" (Matthew 6:33).

The purpose of healing for the Christian should center in the person of Jesus Christ and the advancement of His kingdom. God wants us to be healthy and free from pain, but more than that, He wants us to be like Him—to have His mind and His desires in us. God created us that we might bring glory and joy to himself. Until we grasp that truth and make it a practical part of our Christian walk, we run the risk of "asking amiss." "When you ask, you do not receive, because you ask with wrong motives, that you may spend what you get on your pleasures" (James 4:3, *NIV*). Healing does not seem to be excluded from this admonition. Unless our walk with God is close and continual, we may not fully comprehend our own motives in asking for anything from God.

Healing Through the Atonement

As Jesus began His earthly ministry, He identified its nature by quoting Isaiah 61:1, 2: "The Spirit of the Lord is upon me, because he hath anointed me to preach the gospel to the poor; he hath sent me to heal the brokenhearted, to preach deliverance to the captives, and recovering of sight to the blind" (Luke 4:18).

His purpose in coming to earth was to deliver His creation from the bondage of Satan and from the effects that bondage has caused. He came to "destroy him who holds the power of death—that is, the devil—and free those who all their lives were held in slavery by their fear of death" (Hebrews 2:14, 15, *NIV*). The healings and miracles of Jesus were signs that Satan's kingdom was being crushed, that evil, sin, and sickness were to be destroyed by the sacrificial death of Christ.

Since we are redeemed and delivered from the curse of sin and the works of Satan through the death of Christ on the cross, and since sickness is part of the curse of sin, it follows that healing or the conquest of sickness flows from Christ's redemptive work. Both body and soul were contaminated by the Fall. Christ's death provided restoration for both in spiritual and physical healing.

Although the provision of healing was part of the atoning death of Jesus Christ ("With his stripes we are healed"—Isaiah 53:5), there is an even stronger affirmation of healing in the resurrection of Christ. The death of Christ destroyed sin, the root of sickness. But the resurrection life of Jesus provides health and life for our redeemed bodies: "If the Spirit of him that raised up Christ from the dead dwell in you, he that raised up Christ from the dead shall also quicken your mortal bodies by his Spirit that dwelleth in you" (Romans 8:11). The promise is for now as well as for the Resurrection morning.

The Provision for Inner Healing

The spiritual healing of salvation and the physical healing of the body are understood by most Christians, but there is another healing or deliverance that is frequently overlooked, leaving the sufferer in a bondage often greater than that of physical suffering. A whole new area of human problems, the emotions and feelings, has been given great attention by psychologists, counselors, and psychiatrists. Even Christians are the victims of abnormal fears and mental or emotional stresses which Christ desires to dispel through the application of His atoning work at Calvary. Our minds can be free from debilitating fear; if they are not, there is healing for this need. The source of fear is certainly not God. "God hath not given us the spirit of fear; but of power, and of love, and of a sound mind" (2 Timothy 1:7).

Christians who are suffering with sickness sometimes are in need of two healings. They need deliverance from the sickness itself. But they also need deliverance from the fear of what the sickness may lead to if God's healing is not experienced. The fear of permanent confinement in a wheelchair or bed of affliction and the fear of death at the end of the doctor's diagnosis of "terminal illness" can be replaced by quiet trust in God's Word and His promise of healing.

There are also emotional scars that Christians carry needlessly. The pressures of life's complexities, from childhood through adulthood, leave some people emotionally ill and unable to cope with the normal demands of interpersonal relationships. God says to the emotionally ill and to those beset by today's pressures, "I am the Lord that healeth thee" (Exodus 15:26). Even memories that lie buried in the subconscious can be healed by the work of the Holy Spirit.

The Means of Healing

The apostle John, himself the victim of persecution and imprisonment, expressed his strong desire that the readers of his third epistle would be healthy and prosperous: "Beloved, I wish above all things that thou mayest prosper and be in health, even as thy soul prospereth" (3 John 2). But the heart of Jesus, our Great High Priest who is touched by the feeling of our infirmities (Hebrews 4:15), wants us to be healthy even more certainly than John or any relative or friend ever could.

Why then doesn't He heal all who desire to be healed? Various hindrances to healing have been suggested: doubting God's promises, wrong motives, trusting in personal merit, rebellion, failure to care for the body properly, lack of prayer or fasting, and negative fixation on the symptoms. But each of these hindrances can be placed within the all-encompassing reason for which healing is not received: lack of faith. On the occasion when the disciples could not help the lad whose father had brought him to the disciples for healing, Jesus put His finger on the problem, "O faithless generation" (Mark 9:19).

Faith in the Christian Community

Human nature seeks to place the blame for any failure or lack. The failure to appropriate divine healing is no exception. Many a suffering saint has been subjected to the well-intentioned diagnosis of a fortunately healthy observer: "Your faith is too small." But only God knows whose lack of faith is responsible for the delay of healing.

Paul tells us that when one member of the Body suffers, all members suffer with it and when one member is honored, all the members rejoice with it (1 Corinthians 12:26).

The invitation to complete submission, to seek first the kingdom of God, is extended to every generation, but priorities are too frequently inverted. Things which in themselves are legitimate can nevertheless usurp the rightful priority of the Kingdom. In this circumstance, the body of Christ is beset by a wavering of faith (James 1:6). Verbal affirmation is still strong, but unexpressed questions in the minds of many prevent the unified response of corporate faith which has characterized the supernatural moves of the Spirit.

Each of us individually is a member of the Christian community, the body of Christ. We must share in the responsibility for each member of the Body. If we truly desire to see miracles of healing, we must be willing as a Body to pay a price in setting spiritual priorities in correct order.

Not Faith in Faith, but Faith in Jesus

Many are the sick who are waiting for the ministry of the Body in their behalf. Faith is the key. Yet we sometimes stress faith in such a way that this beautiful gift of God is viewed as a spiritual charm or formula to be invoked when there is a need for healing. Faith becomes something that Christians work at or activate in order to persuade God to do something for them.

But faith is the description of a relationship. For the Christian, it is a relationship to Jesus Christ. Faith is a strong confidence in three things: what God is (Psalm 104:1-5), what He has done (126:3), and what He has said (119:89).

Jesus Christ, as the incarnation of what God is, what He has done, and what He has said, is the Object of our faith. As we come to know Him more intimately, our faith in Him grows, and the result of that God-imparted faith is the supernatural visitation of God himself.

Appropriating Our Healing

Healing results from the exercise of divinely initiated faith. Genuine faith that marks the intervention of God in human existence has been and will always be a supernatural gift that comes into the believer's life. The origin, operation, and effect of that faith is "according as God hath dealt to every man the measure of faith" (Romans 12:3).

But God has ordained some steps for His children to follow in order to move into that position where God can impart faith for the healing.

1. Call for the support and ministry of the spiritual leaders in the local congregation. "Is any sick among you? let him call for the elders of the church; and let them pray

over him, anointing him with oil in the name of the Lord" (James 5:14).

2. Humbly strive for personal righteousness and minister to the needs of others in the body of Christ. "Confess your faults one to another, and pray one for another, that ye may be healed. The effectual fervent prayer of a righteous man availeth much" (James 5:16).

3. Give God the opportunity to plant faith through the study and appropriation of the Word. "Faith cometh by hearing, and hearing by the word of God" (Romans 10:17).

Victory Over Suffering—Until the Healing Comes

The overwhelming message of Scripture concerning divine healing is clear. It is God's nature to heal. God loves us, and through the identification of Jesus Christ with the human race, He understands and feels the pain and suffering we experience. Healing has been provided in the death and resurrection of Christ. Promise after promise throughout Scripture assures us that God can and will heal. Everyone who places his trust in Jesus can be healed. This truth we must affirm with complete confidence if we are to receive healing.

Yet we observe Christians suffering from physical affliction and infirmity. As we have seen earlier, judgment or the placing of blame by other Christians is wrong. The one who suffers should certainly check his own relationship with God to see if there is something that should be corrected. After such self-examination, what does the sufferer do if healing does not come? Does He question God and doubt the promises of His infallible Word?

This is the point of greatest test for the suffering believer. He must never let go of the confidence that God will heal him. But he lives with pain or affliction that makes unwavering faith a difficult task, especially in his own strength. He must continually affirm his belief that God is his Healer, and at the same time he must remain faithful, expecting the healing after God's reason for delay has been accomplished. Should the healing never come, his faith and that of fellow Christians must stand firm in the assurance that Sovereign God is accomplishing higher purposes that He chooses not to share with them. But through it all, the suffering Christian knows that God heals and that he is learning to trust in God because of the experience.

Although God's Word does not explain why healing does not always come the moment it is requested, it does describe the life of faithfulness that waits patiently for the healing.

1. Pray and enjoy communion with God. "Is any among you afflicted? let him pray" (James 5:13).

2. Walk in obedience to the Word of God. "Thou shalt therefore keep the commandments, and the statutes, and the judgments, which I command thee. . . . And the Lord will take away from thee all sickness" (Deuteronomy 7:11, 15).

3. Wait upon the Lord for His strength. "He giveth power to the faint; and to them that have no might he increaseth strength. . . . They that wait upon the Lord shall renew their strength" (Isaiah 40:29, 31).

4. Be encouraged in God's faithfulness. "Wherefore lift up the hands which hang down, and the feeble knees; and make straight paths for your feet, lest that which is lame be turned out of the way; but let it rather be healed" (Hebrews 12:12, 13).

* * * * *

Thank God for His provision of healing. Yet at its best, it is only a restoration to a better plane in a human life of frailty, suffering, and eventually physical death unless Jesus comes before that time.

But we look forward to a time when there will be no healing—when there will be *no need* for healing. All will be perfect and whole. John saw that future day as the time when "there shall be no more curse" (Revelation 22:3). Thank God for His provision of healing in the present order of things, but we pray with desire, "Hasten, Lord, the day when healing is no longer needed."

7

Teaching the Truths of Divine Healing

Cardinal Doctrine Three

"Divine healing is not giving up medicines," said A. B. Simpson, "or fighting with physicians, or against remedies. It is not even believing in prayer, or the prayer of faith, or in the men and women who teach divine healing. It is not even believing the doctrine to be true. But it is really receiving the personal life of Christ to be in us as the supernatural strength of our body and the supply of our physical life. It is a living fact and not a mere theory or doctrine."

Your task as a teacher is to lead your students beyond the theory or doctrine to the appropriation of the life and strength of Christ in our physical bodies.

Understanding Divine Healing

Children are usually the epitome of health and physical vitality. If they have a personal interest in divine healing, it is usually through the sickness of a parent or grandparent. But the seed of faith in the healing power of Jesus Christ should be planted at an early age. If the lesson is well learned as a child, trust in God during a later physical crisis will come much more naturally.

The Divine Pattern of Growth and Health

"Jesus increased in wisdom and stature, and in favor

with God and man" (Luke 2:52). This verse says that Jesus grew in the normal fashion, just like all young children. His mind expanded and He could comprehend more complex ideas. His body developed through exercise and eating nourishing food. He must have been a pleasant and polite young man, well-liked by the people who knew Him. Most of all, His perfect obedience to His Heavenly Father gave Him increasing favor with God. The similarities between the growth and development of Jesus and our total development are seen below:

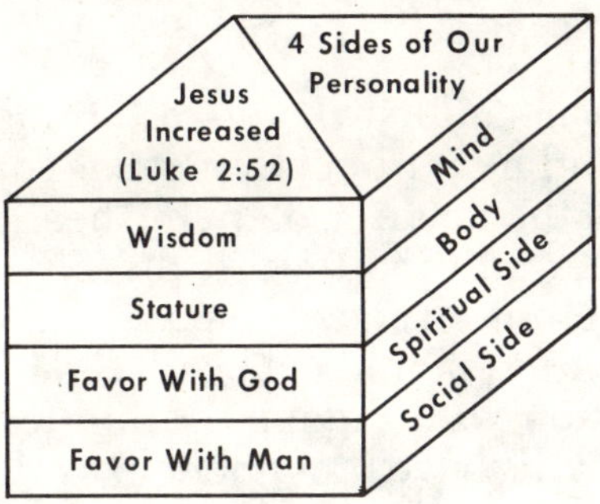

God made man to be a social creature. He ordained the family as a unit in which individual persons could help each other. The church, the school, and the community are larger families or groups in which we must relate to others. God intends that each part of our personality should develop and be healthy. So a healthy body is God's desire for each of His children.

Healing as Part of the Gospel

The Statement of Fundamental Truths of the Assemblies of God states: "Divine healing is an integral part of the gospel. Deliverance from sickness is provided for in the atonement, and is the privilege of all believers (Isaiah 53:4, 5; Matthew 8:16, 17; James 5:14-16)."

Healing was an important part of the earthly ministry of Jesus. His power to heal was a demonstration of His authority to forgive sins (Mark 2:5-12). Jesus recognized that sickness can be the result of sin (John 5:14) or of Satan's work (Luke 13:16). If God were not able to heal, one area of sin's domain would remain unconquered. At Calvary, Christ made a full atonement for the whole man.

Memorize the following verses: Exodus 15:26; Psalm 107:20; Isaiah 53:5; James 5:14, 15.

Healing and the Place of Doctors

There are some adults who do rash things in rejecting all medicine and help from physicians. To guard against future abuse of the doctrine of divine healing, teach children the proper attitude toward the medical advances that God has permitted and even guided men in discovering. Divine healing should not be placed in opposition to or in competition with the medical profession. Doctors through their skills have brought help to many sufferers.

Some people point to the condemnation of King Asa because "in his disease he sought not to the Lord, but to the physicians" (2 Chronicles 16:12). But the emphasis is not on the fact that he sought physicians (who may have been heathen physicians), but that he turned his back on the Lord. He had already refused to rely on the Lord when he turned to Syria for help (2 Chronicles 16:7).

Other Scripture references to physicians are favorable (Jeremiah 8:22; Mark 2:17). Even the reference to physicians in the story of the woman with the issue of blood is not unfavorable. True, she "had suffered many things of many physicians, and had spent all that she had, and was nothing bettered, but rather grew worse" (Mark 5:26). But the woman was not told that it was wrong for her to go to the physicians. They simply had not been able to help her.

Today, God still performs miracles for persons the doctors have declared incurable. If it were wrong to go to physicians, why would God reward disobedience with the miracle of healing? God may allow His children to find health through the means of medicine or through the touch of miraculous healing. But one thing we must avoid: We cannot rely on the skill of man as a *substitute* for seeking the help of God.

Making Divine Healing Relevant

Teenagers, like children, generally know good health. So the challenge to the teacher of teenagers is to make the doctrine of divine healing relevant for their world.

Divine Health and the Care of the Body

God wants us to be well, no matter what our age. He has promised long life to His children who love Him sincerely and obey His Word (Psalm 91:14, 16). Long life is also promised if we obey our parents (Exodus 20:12; Ephesians 6:1-3).

Paul speaks of our bodies as the temples of the Holy Spirit. But some teenagers forget this and treat their bodies carelessly. Even after medical science has positively demonstrated the dangerous effects of smoking, young people still foolishly try to show their "maturity" by experimenting with cigarettes. They endanger their lives and those of others on the highways when they use one of the worst drugs of all—alcohol.

God's miracle of healing can reach a person no matter what physical injury he may have suffered, but we have no right to expect healing if we flagrantly violate the natural laws God has left for our well-being. The same principle applies to gluttony and withholding necessary sleep from our bodies. Divine healing is no substitute for obedience to the rules of physical and mental health.

Memorize the following verses: Exodus 15:26; Deuteronomy 7:15; Hebrews 4:15, 16.

Renewal of the Mind and Body

Teenagers are especially susceptible to the temptations of the mind. The lyrics of popular music and pornography can pollute a mind and even make it sick. Things that start as seemingly harmless flirtations with the mysterious or forbidden can become habits that bind a person as cruelly as any crippling illness. The effects of alcohol and drugs can leave permanent injury and damage.

But the one who comes to Jesus Christ for salvation and deliverance from such sicknesses can know the healing power of Almighty God. The record of recovery from drug addiction by medical and psychological means is pathetically poor. Yet a miracle of divine grace has more than once delivered a trapped teenager from hellish slavery. Your teenagers who have never stooped to abuse their bodies through the use of drugs, alcohol, or cigarettes, can proclaim full deliverance and healing to their acquaintances who have been caught.

Paul summed up the potential for the body and mind of the young person: "I beseech you therefore, brethren, by the mercies of God, that ye present your bodies a living sacrifice, holy, acceptable unto God, which is your reasonable service. And be not conformed to this world: but be ye transformed by the renewing of your mind, that ye may prove what is that good, and acceptable, and perfect will of God" (Romans 12:1, 2). This ideal is not beyond the reach of every teenager, no matter what injury he has suffered, if he gives his life completely to Jesus.

Healing for Attitudes and Emotions

Things don't always go smoothly for teenagers. Nor for adults, either, for that matter. There are so many persons and institutions that seem to thwart the perfect happiness that would certainly come if we could have things the way we would like them to be. Parents, teachers, the employer—these all seem to trespass on the rights and freedoms that just naturally should be claimed. This is a common experience for all human beings. It must have been made a part of our lives by God himself to test the character that really resides within.

We have to be careful that bitterness doesn't creep into our lives. "Watch out that no bitterness takes root among you, for as it springs up it causes deep trouble, hurting many in their spiritual lives" (Hebrews 12:15, *The Living Bible*). We only hurt ourselves when we harbor bitterness.

Many are the young people and adults who carry a heavy load of bitterness, jealousy, or fear. But there is healing for these spiritual afflictions as God is allowed to minister to the inner man. Divine healing will be very relevant to your students if you help them reach out to Christ for His deliverance in this area of their lives.

Appropriating the Truth of Divine Healing

Your task as a teacher is more than explaining how divine healing works or why some people are not healed. You must be a builder of faith. You must impart to your students the unshakable conviction that God does heal. Your attitude as you share God's Word on the subject of divine healing may inspire faith for needed healing.

The Privilege of All Believers

No one in the recorded miracles of healing in Scripture

had the audacity to demand healing. Those who came to Jesus were desperate, but they did not look on healing as their inherent right, but as a gracious privilege.

Just as salvation is by grace through faith (Ephesians 2:8), so the healing ministry of Christ is ours by His grace or unmerited favor. We neither earn nor deserve healing, but God offers it as the privilege of all believers. The fact that it is provided for us does not rule out suffering for the sake of Christ and the gospel. Yet we can boldly claim, in the midst of suffering, that God does heal.

In humility we must admit that we do not understand everything about divine healing. As Paul said, we still see through a glass darkly. We do not know why some are healed and others are not. To presume to know why individual Christians are not healed is to assume wrongly the role of God in judging the spiritual condition of people. Even the New Testament records the martyrdom of James and the deliverance of Peter. Though we cannot understand some of these matters, our responsibility is to preach the Word and expect the signs to follow.

Memorize the following verses: Isaiah 40:29, 31; Romans 8:11; James 5:16.

Special Concerns of the Aged

Divine healing is not a means of avoiding the effects of old age. The gradual deterioration of our bodies (graphically described in Ecclesiastes 12:1-7), is experienced by believers as well as unbelievers. Healing is certainly available to the aged, just as it is for those in the prime of life. But the part of the body that is healed usually continues to age like the rest of the body. We do not yet have the completed resurrection redemption of the body. No matter what we do for this body, no matter how many healings we experience, if Jesus tarries we shall all die.

The realities of old age and physical decline do not negate the truth of divine healing. Nor should they discourage us from seeking and expecting healing at any stage of life. Even though the outward man is perishing, the inward man can be renewed day by day (2 Corinthians 4:16). Divine healing or health, though certainly God's desire for us, is not the highest priority Christ has ordained for believers. He seeks first to make us into His spiritual likeness.

The Ministry of the Holy Spirit in Healing

"But if the Spirit of him that raised up Jesus from the dead dwell in you, he that raised up Christ from the dead shall also quicken your mortal bodies by his Spirit that dwelleth in you" (Romans 8:11). It was through Christ's death that healing was provided, and the Spirit ministers the healing to us. What complete comfort this Comforter brings!

Gifts of healing are among the manifestations of the Spirit which are provided for the edification and strengthening of the Church (1 Corinthians 12:7, 9). Like the other gifts, healings are administered through members of the Body. But the operation of the gift through a believer does not make him a healer. Just as the operation of the word of wisdom does not make the inspired speaker a perpetually wise man, so it is with the gifts of healing. God is the source of the wisdom and of the healing. A fresh gift of healing must be given by the Spirit for each individual need.

Your responsibility as a teacher in dealing with the truth of divine healing is great. Spend time in intimate fellowship with Jesus Christ, and the believing faith that results in your heart will spill over into the lives of those who have need for a healing of the body.

8

The Glorious Hope of His Coming

Cardinal Doctrine Four

"And so shall we ever be with the Lord" (1 Thessalonians 4:17).

Nine glorious words, unsurpassed in meaning for the Christian! Complete restoration . . . permanently . . . forever!

When we stand in the very presence of Jesus himself, the story of salvation, of God's dealing with man, will be complete. The perfect fellowship for which we were created will be restored—never to be interrupted again.

"Therefore encourage each other with these words" (1 Thessalonians 4:18, *NIV*).

Living in the Last Days

Signs of the Time

Having been told that the present order of things would come to an end, the disciples asked Jesus the two questions that have intrigued many minds since then: "When shall these things be? and what shall be the sign of thy coming, and of the end of the world?" (Matthew 24:3).

We need not be taken by surprise at the return of Jesus. The Day of the Lord will slip up as a thief on those who are unprepared. But Christians, with God-given discernment, should be watching and ready. A study of Matthew

24:4-38 will reveal between 25 and 30 signs. The most prominent are the appearance of deceivers (v. 5), wars and rumors of wars (v. 6), famine (v. 7), pestilences (v. 7), earthquakes in many places (v. 7), persecution (v. 9), hatred (v. 10), false prophets (v. 11), signs and wonders by counterfeit persons (v. 24), sun and moon darkened (v. 29), and people living carelessly as in the days of Noah (v. 38).

The end times will be full of frightening happenings. Christians will be spared from suffering some of them by being taken in the Rapture. But we will not escape them all, and Christ gave warning and instruction on how to live in the last days (Matthew 24).

1. Take heed that no man deceive you (v. 4).
2. Don't be troubled or alarmed at the signs (v. 6).
3. Stand firm until the end (v. 13).
4. Preach the gospel in all the world (v. 14).
5. Be ready to flee from evil and persecution (vv. 16-19).
6. Understand from the signs that Christ's coming and the end are near (v. 33).
7. Watch continually for His coming (v. 42).
8. Be ready spiritually for His coming (v. 44).
9. Be a faithful and wise servant (vv. 45, 46).

Do our lives agree with our verbal affirmation that Jesus could come at any time? There is no sign, either in Matthew 24 or elsewhere in the Bible, distinctly placed before the Rapture, that has not yet been seen. The end of life as we know it today could be very soon.

The Delay of Christ's Coming

If all the signs of Christ's coming have already been witnessed in some fashion, why doesn't the Rapture take place immediately? The born-again child of God asks that question as he anticipates the wonderful event. Sinners and scoffers, however, interpret the delay in another manner: "There shall come in the last days scoffers, walking after their own lusts, and saying, Where is the promise of his coming? for since the fathers fell asleep, all things continue as they were from the beginning of the creation" (2 Peter 3:3, 4). Peter then proceeds to give two reasons for the delay.

1. God measures time differently than man does. "One day is with the Lord as a thousand years, and a thousand years as one day" (2 Peter 3:8).

2. God delays His coming because He desires that more will come to repentance through His patience. "It is not that the Lord is slow in fulfilling his promise, as some suppose, but that he is very patient with you, because it is not his will for any to be lost, but for all to come to repentance" (2 Peter 3:9, *NEB*).

The Rapture

The study of prophecy must be translated into personal meaning. The truth of Christ's return should be more than just a future event. It should be a blessed hope for each Christian. How it will affect those who are not ready should make each Christian a more compassionate and effective witness.

First Phase of the Second Coming

Jesus Christ is the central figure of prophecy, just as He is the central figure of the entire Bible. To the Christian who truly loves Jesus, the sudden appearance of Christ in the air will hold no fear, dread, or disappointment. The words of Paul concerning this beginning of end-time events should summarize the anticipation of all real "Jesus people": "Looking for that blessed hope, and the glorious appearing of the great God and our Saviour Jesus Christ" (Titus 2:13).

Many Christians lack a clear understanding of the second coming of Christ. When we say that the next event in God's timetable of history is the Second Coming, we are using the term in a general sense that includes the rapture of the saints as the first phase of the Second Coming. At this time, Christ comes and snatches away His church, without actually setting foot on the earth. With the saints removed from the earth, the Great Tribulation comes upon the whole world. At the end of this great period of suffering, Christ returns *with* His saints to confront the Antichrist and his forces at the battle of Armageddon. Since this is the time when Christ physically appears on earth, as He did at the time of His first coming, this event is more exactly the Second Coming to earth, or the Revelation of Jesus Christ. The "Panorama of Prophecy" chart will make the relation between these events more easily understood.

PANORAMA OF PROPHECY

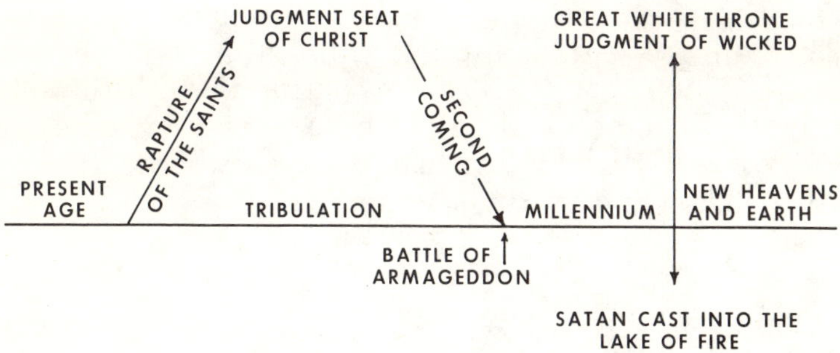

Although there are references throughout the New Testament to the rapture of the saints, two passages describe it in the best detail: "For the Lord himself shall descend from heaven with a shout, with the voice of the archangel, and with the trump of God: and the dead in Christ shall rise first: then we which are alive and remain shall be caught up together with them in the clouds, to meet the Lord in the air: and so shall we ever be with the Lord" (1 Thessalonians 4:16, 17).

"We shall all be changed, in a moment, in the twinkling of an eye, at the last trump: for the trumpet shall sound, and the dead shall be raised incorruptible, and we shall be changed" (1 Corinthians 15:51, 52).

Changed Bodies

If the dead in Christ are resurrected with incorruptible bodies at the Rapture, the new bodies will be far different from the old bodies. According to 1 Corinthians 15:52, the bodies of the living saints will be changed too. Natural curiosity causes us to ask what they will be like.

The Bible does not give a complete description of the new bodies. The full revelation will be a glorious surprise. We get just a peek in the Gospel accounts of Jesus after His resurrection and in 1 Corinthians 15:41-54. These things we do know about the resurrection body:

1. The new body will have continuity with the old body like a plant which grows from a seed (vv. 42-44).
2. We will still be individuals in our new bodies (v. 41).
3. Our new bodies will be perfect (v. 49).

Beginning of the Day of the Lord

The frequency with which the phrase *the Day of the Lord* occurs in Scripture gives evidence of its importance in prophecy. But there has been disagreement among scholars as to its specific meaning. Some apply it to the Tribulation only, for judgment against evil is prominent in the Biblical description of the day.

Paul tells us that "the day of the Lord so cometh as a

thief in the night" (1 Thessalonians 5:2). It seems most appropriate therefore to define the Day of the Lord as that period, at the end of this present age, when God's dealing with Israel, Satan's kingdom, and His own children is intensified and consummated. It begins with the Rapture and the tribulation period and extends through the Millennium into the new heavens and earth.

The Great Tribulation

The Tribulation is a period of 7 years, the "70th week" of Daniel (Daniel 9:27). The last half of the tribulation period is referred to as the Great Tribulation. *Pre-Tribulation* advocates believe that the Rapture will occur before the beginning of Daniel's 70th week. *Mid-Tribulation* advocates believe the Rapture will occur in the middle of the 70th week, or before the Great Tribulation. *Post-Tribulation* advocates believe the Rapture will occur at the end of the 70th week, or when Christ comes to set up His kingdom.

The Tribulation directly concerns Israel and is God's judgment for long apostasy and neglect of the Messiah. The Tribulation also affects the whole world because of its ungodliness and ill treatment of the Jews. The first half of these final 7 years will probably be a time of prosperity and acceptance of the Antichrist as the great deliverer from economic chaos. But the latter part of the period will witness the plagues described in Revelation.

The Role of the Antichrist

When will the Antichrist appear? What will he be like? and what will he do? The Bible warns against false christs or men who claim to be the Messiah or Deliverer. But this antichrist is *the Antichrist* because he will be Satan's special representative from the pit.

Daniel 9:27 contains what can be known about Antichrist's activity. The rest must be speculation and interpretation. "He shall confirm the covenant with many for one week: and in the midst of the week he shall cause the sacrifice and the oblation to cease." The week corresponds with the 7 years of the Tribulation; the middle of the week with the Great Tribulation or last half of the week. The covenant seems to refer to an agreement between the Jews and the Antichrist which permits the resumption of ancient sacrificial worship. When the agreement is repudiated, the time of Jacob's Trouble (Jeremiah 30:7) will begin. The Antichrist will turn on the Jews, and only Jesus' return to earth, with His saints, will defeat the Antichrist and deliver Israel.

Events on Earth

Bible students have noted in the Biblical references to Satan, the Antichrist, and the False Prophet, a satanic trinity. The evil three carry out their devilish designs against God and Israel in an attempt to destroy the kingdom of righteousness. The three are ultimately consigned to the lake of fire.

But God is still in control. His patience with evil men who choose to follow Satan finally fills to the full and spills out on the earth as the wrath of a righteous God. Seven trumpets announce plagues of judgment: hail and fire mingled with blood, part of the sea turned to blood, the water made bitter, part of the celestial bodies darkened, locusts that torment with severe pain, earthquakes, and death to many people (Revelation 8 and 9). Further plagues are poured out from the vials of God's wrath: ulcers and sores on men, seas and rivers turned to blood, the earth scorched by the heat of the sun, darkness, the Euphrates River dried up, the earth shaken, and land features changed (Revelation 16).

How will this unbelievable destruction and carnage end? The unholy trinity will lead the kings of the earth into preparing for war against God. The battle array will be in the Valley of Jezreel, near the site of Megiddo. Suddenly, Christ will appear, accompanied by a heavenly army of saints and angels. For these there is no death; the battle is completely one-sided. The outcome is so obvious that even before the battle commences, God calls the vultures of the world for a feast.

"The Lord shall consume [Antichrist] with the spirit of his mouth, and shall destroy [him] with the brightness of his coming" (2 Thessalonians 2:8). The host accompanying Christ increase the grandeur, but do not fight the battle. Christ himself will destroy five-sixths of the assembled forces at Armageddon—with His word and the brightness of His presence. We are on the winning side.

Events in Heaven

The rapture of the Church marks the beginning of events in heaven for the saints, while God's wrath is being poured out on the earth. First is our summons to the *Judgment Seat of Christ* where our works will be judged. This will be the highest court to which the Christian is ever called, for he has previously been judged by his acceptance of the work accomplished on the Cross. His bad works are not sins, for those have been judged earlier. The good and bad deeds are those worthy of reward and the worthless ones. As we stand before the judgment seat, these principles will be noted:

1. God gives credit to the planter and waterer, as well as to the reaper.
2. God sees the sacrifice of our labor, not the amount.
3. Our judgment will take into consideration how we have judged others (Matthew 7:1).

4. Faithfulness is given first priority.
5. Our motives will be judged at this time. What we do now counts for eternity (2 Corinthians 5:10, 11).

After we have been judged, we are ready to be presented as the perfect bride of Christ, arrayed in the "righteousness of saints" (Revelation 19:8). The marriage of the Church and the Lamb, the focus of so much Biblical imagery and comparison, is finally consummated. After the wedding, of course, follows the Marriage Supper of the Lamb.

The Revelation or Second Coming of Christ

The real second coming of Christ is the visible, bodily appearance of Christ as He returns to the Mount of Olives from which He ascended after His resurrection. This is the second phase of the Second Coming which had its beginning at the rapture of the dead and living believers. In order for the Lord to come *with* His saints (Revelation 19:14), they must previously have been gathered to Him. We therefore speak quite correctly of the first and second phases of the Second Coming.

The Manner of the Revelation

After the marriage between the saints and the Lamb in heaven, the Groom goes forth to claim all of His kingdom. He rides on a white horse, followed by the saints, also on white horses (Revelation 19:11, 14). He is also accompanied by the angels as He comes in His glory (Matthew 25:31).

The extent to which the description in Revelation 19:11-16 is literal or symbolic will be known by firsthand experience as the blood-washed saints follow their King in the procession. But it is certain to be a sight of great wonder and majesty as Christ descends with the splendor of flashing lightning to claim that which Satan has temporarily wrested from His hand.

Armageddon—The Conflict of the Worlds

This is not science fiction. It is a climactic struggle between God and the principalities and powers of darkness. When these two worlds collide, the foundations of the earth will be shaken. All men and women will be affected.

"The kings of the earth and of the whole world" (Revelation 16:14) are brought together by the unholy trinity to a place called Armageddon (v. 16). It is here that God pours out judgment on the nations for their persecution of Israel and for their general sinfulness and godlessness. The battle will probably spread over much of the land of Palestine. Revelation describes the blood flowing to the horses' bridles for 1,600 furlongs. Christ and His army are victorious.

Satan Bound

The significance of this "battle of that great day of God Almighty" is not in the number killed or in the amount of blood shed. It is in the spiritual victory accomplished when Satan is bound and cast into the bottomless pit (Revelation 20:3), so that he can no longer deceive the nations and people as he has done for centuries. For the first time since Lucifer rebelled and fell from heaven, every hostile force that would challenge Christ's rule over the earth will be suppressed. The other two members of the unholy trinity are at this time cast into the lake of fire from which there is no release.

The Millennium; New Heavens and Earth

With Satan's influence removed from the earth and

Christ's reign of righteousness unopposed, the Millennium will be a time of unsurpassed glory and perfect relationships. References to this future state of perfection are found throughout the Scriptures. The Old Testament prophets anticipated the day when Israel would again fill a special place of prominence and blessing. The Christian today, tired of the pain and suffering of the curse, also anticipates this time of peace and joy. Some of the more significant characteristics of the Millennium should not be overlooked.

1. Christ's rule will be over the entire earth (Daniel 7:14), absolute in authority and power (Isaiah 11:4), and completely righteous and just (Isaiah 11:3-5).
2. Israel will enjoy special privileges, although the Gentiles who recognize Christ as Lord will be active participants and receive blessings as well.
3. The curse on the earth will be lifted during the Millennium (Isaiah 35).
4. The normally aggressive nature of animals will be changed (Isaiah 11).
5. Health, healing, and long life will be evident (Isaiah 35 and 65).
6. The Mount of Olives and the adjacent land surface will be supernaturally modified (Zechariah 14).
7. Jerusalem will become the capital city of the entire world (Isaiah 60:12, 14).

The above description of the Millennium and Christ's earthly kingdom emphasizes a material kingdom instead of a spiritual one. In the Millennium, Christ's kingdom will be both physical and spiritual. Here are some of the spiritual characteristics of that Kingdom.

8. The truth of God will be widespread, "as the waters cover the sea" (Isaiah 11).

9. Righteousness, obedience, and holiness will characterize the Kingdom (Isaiah 62; Zechariah 14).
10. There will be universal peace (Isaiah 2).
11. There will be great joy and happiness (Isaiah 12).
12. The Millennium will be a time of real fullness of the Spirit (Isaiah 32).

This is what Christ's second coming will bring to the earth. May God hasten the day.

The Final Fate of Satan

The Millennium is not forever, just 1,000 years. Then there must be another fine tuning in God's end-time dealing with the earth and its inhabitants before the perfection of eternity begins. During the Millennium there will be normal family relationships with children born to husbands and wives. Before the 1,000 years are completed, the children thus born will far outnumber their parents. Some of them will have obeyed Christ only "because everyone is doing it." Satan's release will be their test of love, faith, and loyalty.

Revelation 20:3 describes the release of Satan for "a little season." One last time, Satan will deceive the nations and gather together a group of rebels to oppose God. He and his followers will do battle with Christ and His faithful. This rebellion will be short-lived. Fire will come down from heaven and devour the opposition. Satan will finally be cast into the lake of fire permanently.

The Great White Throne Judgment

This is the saddest scene in the entire Bible. After the judgment fire physically destroys those deceived by Satan at the end of the Millennium, all of the wicked who have ever lived on the face of the earth will be dead. Then will follow the resurrection of the wicked dead to stand before the austere Judge "from whose face the earth and the heaven fled away" (Revelation 20:11). The books are opened and they are judged according to their works. Then, like Satan, they will be consigned to the lake of fire to be tormented day and night forever.

If we really grasp the power of the scene that awaits the sinner at the Great White Throne Judgment, we will be moved to do what we can to help him escape this tragic end. Although the wicked deserve what they get, we should not delight in their end. God certainly does not. Our reaction should be one of compassion which, like God's, desires their salvation.

The Holy City

Revelation 20 ends with the Great White Throne Judgment. Chapter 21 begins with John's view of a new heaven and a new earth; the holy city, the new Jerusalem is coming down from God out of the new heavens to rest on the new earth.

To find out how the new heaven and earth come about, we must compare this passage in Revelation with Isaiah 65:17 and 2 Peter 3:10-13. Peter gives the best details on how it will happen: "The heavens shall pass away with a great noise, and the elements shall melt with fervent heat" (3:10).

The Bible says nothing more about the origin of the city than that it comes "from God out of heaven." From Revelation 21 and 22 we glean the following evidence of its majesty, either symbolic or real: crystal clear light; precious stones in the walls; pure, transparent gold construction; a pure river supporting a virtual paradise; and perpetual divine light. But even more significant is what will be missing from the city: tears, death, sorrow, pain, evil persons, night, and the curse man had previously lived under.

The description of eternity with Christ ends here. And rightly so! We are just introduced to the excitement and magnificence of the forever and ever. Only at that time will we see and hear that which we are told we cannot now grasp: "Eye hath not seen, nor ear heard, neither have entered into the heart of man, the things which God hath prepared for them that love him" (1 Corinthians 2:9).

In the "Hallelujah Chorus" of his oratorio *The Messiah*, George Frederick Handel caught some of the overwhelming joy and anticipation that should come to the Christian as he contemplates the glorious time he will share with the Father, the Son, and the Spirit.

The Lord God Omnipotent reigneth!
Hallelujah! Hallelujah!

9

Teaching the Truths of the Second Coming

Cardinal Doctrine Four

The Sunday school superintendent stood before the school and read the Easter story. His voice was strong and composed, even though, as the listeners knew, he had lost his two little children just a week earlier to the dread diphtheria. Many in the audience were weeping, but the superintendent and his wife remained serene and calm.

"How can they do it?" one listener asked of his neighbor, "it's unbelievable."

"They must really believe the whole bit about Easter, the Resurrection, and heaven," said one observer, nodding his head in disbelief.

"Well, of course. All Christians believe in that."

"But not like the superintendent and his wife. They really believe it."

Of course the young couple felt the loss and the grief, the emptiness of a quiet home. But they had a trust that sustained them and made them a blessing to others even while they suffered. They knew there would one day be a resurrection and they looked forward to the coming of Jesus when that resurrection will take place.

Understanding the Second Coming

Many adults live in the here and now—for today, not

next week or next year. How then can the teacher present the truth of the Second Coming, of heaven and end-time events, so as to gain from students a hearing for these important future happenings?

Emotional Responses to the Message

Different people react differently to the truth that Jesus Christ is coming to earth again. Some are *frightened*. (The faces can be drawn on the chalkboard or on paper plates and used along with the corresponding explanations.) They close their eyes and ears to the events of the news that remind them how bad things are in the world and that Jesus has to come soon because we already see so many of the signs mentioned throughout the Bible. Yet they do nothing to get ready to meet Him.

Other people seem *unconcerned* when someone tells them that Jesus is coming soon and that those who are not ready will be judged and punished. If things are going well for them now, they are satisfied to let the future take care of itself. These are the people who never plan ahead. They live only for the fun and enjoyment of the present. They are sleeping when they should be awake and

watching for the great event that could take place at any time.

But others are like this man. Even though everything around him seems dark and threatening, even though there is trouble and persecution everywhere, even though it seems like the economy may crumble, the country be defeated, and the whole world destroyed by a nuclear war, this man wears a smile on his face. He has *joy.* There is a song in his heart because Jesus is coming soon, and the troubles of this world will then be over for him. There are many different responses to the promise of Christ's coming, but the Christian should know only one: "And when these things begin to come to pass, then look up, and lift up your heads; for your redemption draweth nigh" (Luke 21:28).

Looking Forward to Heaven

What for a child is so exciting about heaven? What can he do with streets of gold? He can play baseball on grass or asphalt just as well as on gold. Yet the teacher must present heaven so it is attractive to children.

I believe there will be streets of gold in heaven. The Bible says so. But if I get there and find out that the description is an image to help me understand what a beautiful place it will be, I won't be disappointed. The most important thing for any Christian should be the real presence of Jesus himself. "So shall we ever be with the Lord" (1 Thessalonians 4:17).

Streets of gold would have special meaning for adults who have struggled for years to earn sufficient money to provide food, shelter, and clothing for a growing family. Gold so plentiful that you walk on it rather than spend it to buy the necessities of life! The struggle for the basic essentials of life will be over. Heavenly streets of gold is an excellent way to speak of the day when troubles and trials will be behind.

But what does that mean to children who still enjoy the benefits provided by parents—parents who sacrifice everything that their young ones might be spared as long as possible from the hard realities of life? Yet you can describe heaven for children to make it as appealing as it is for tired adults. Isaiah said it first, then Paul quoted it many years later: "But as it is written, Eye hath not seen, nor ear heard, neither have entered into the heart of man, the things which God hath prepared for them that love him" (1 Corinthians 2:9). The application can be made to spiritual blessings now, but how much greater are the things He is preparing for us in heaven!

How can you impart this anticipation of heaven to children? By relating the joy of heaven to the greatest pleasure their young hearts can imagine now. Ask your class: "What do you like to do more than anything else? What would you ask for if you could have anything you wanted in the whole world; and how would you feel when it was given to you?" Don't try to spiritualize these questions at this point. You are trying to impart the "feel" of heaven; the literal explanation will come later. One class of boys decided that they would rather play baseball than anything else. Four months later, of course, it would have been football.

"How would you like to play a game of cosmic baseball?" the teacher asked. "The earth could be home plate, Mars first base, Jupiter second base, Saturn third base. Little Mercury could be the baseball. Batter up!"

The boys were excited. That kind of a baseball game would make the sandlot game rather tame.

"You can play all the cosmic baseball you want to in heaven." The teacher didn't tell the boys though that in heaven they would rather do other things. But at this stage in their spiritual development, resting or visiting with Jesus didn't yet have an appeal.

In another class was a junior boy from a large family of limited means. He was asked what he would request when he got to heaven. "The first thing I'd like is a hot chocolate sundae and then I'd like to see Jesus." The theology wasn't too good, but the "feel" of heaven had entered his consciousness.

In both of the instances above, the next step of explanation was important. "You may not play cosmic baseball or eat hot chocolate sundaes in heaven, but whatever you do will be even more enjoyable than those experiences. Because Jesus will be there, it will be an exciting place."

Memorize the following verses: John 14:2, 3; 1 Thessalonians 4:16-18.

Making the Second Coming Relevant

Can't Jesus Wait a While?

One young teenager confided tearfully to her mother, "I don't want Jesus to come until after I get married and have a family." The truth of the Second Coming had lodged in her heart. She loved the Lord with her whole heart, but the beautiful things of life also had an attraction. With love, her mother assured her that Jesus would do what was just right for her. She could plan to be part of her own Christian family, and plan it with Jesus. If He should come before she married, He would still allow her to experience the same feelings of joy and happiness that the fulfillment of her Christian family plans would bring.

Teenagers should learn that Christ's coming for His children is not an interruption or an end to the enjoyable things of life. It is the capstone or fulfillment of a life completely dedicated to Him in every detail. How many young people, openly or inwardly, hope that Jesus will not come for a while yet. They know from their elders that they should desire His coming, and they give lip service to the idea, but they do have their reservations. As their teacher, you should teach them a balanced appreciation for the here and the hereafter.

Memorize the following verses: Matthew 16:27; 24:14, 44; Acts 1:11.

But It Could Be Today

Other young people don't want Jesus to return because they are not ready for His coming. They are not living right, and they want to taste all the pleasures of the world before settling down to get ready.

It doesn't work that way, though. The very things that attract and entice now will become obstacles and hindrances when the mind starts to turn toward the righteous life. "Behold, now is the accepted time; behold, now is the day of salvation" (2 Corinthians 6:2).

Prophecy and Front-page News

There is one good way of making the Second Coming relevant for your teenagers. But it requires work on your part. You must become a student of the end times. When the newspapers report widespread famine, devastating earthquakes, and other natural catastrophes, you have a perfect opportunity to ask: "What is God saying to us through this happening? Is He trying to tell us to be ready, for His coming is getting very near?"

Making the Second Coming a Blessed Hope

It is not just scoffers and skeptics who say: "Where is this 'coming' he promised? . . . Everything goes on as it has since the beginning of creation" (2 Peter 3:4, *NIV*). Many Christians give lip service to the truth of the Second Coming but then live with a carelessness or preoccupation with earthly concerns that betrays a faded expectation of the Lord's return. The teacher of adults must strive to make the Second Coming an imminent event that is viewed with anticipation.

This Could Be the Crowning Day

In John 14 we see the concept of heaven and man's difficulty in grasping its reality. To the disciples Jesus said, "I will come again, and receive you unto myself; that where I am, there ye may be also" (v. 3). That speaks of heaven. But Thomas answered, "We know not whither thou goest; and how can we know the way?" (v. 5). To know the place where Jesus is (heaven), is to know Jesus and desire to be with Him.

The disciples had spent 3½ years with Jesus. Now that He was about to leave them, they would miss Him. But they didn't have that overwhelming desire to be with Jesus, wherever He might be going. What they needed was an understanding of the true meaning of heaven.

Like the disciples, we need to be possessed with an overwhelming desire to be with Jesus. Our first desire, as the things of earth fade at the brightness of Christ's presence, should be an intense desire to see Jesus, to run to His bosom. When that feeling burns in our hearts, the reality of heaven has come alive.

Like Thomas, we do not know the place (to be with Jesus), so we find it hard to understand the way (to view heaven with anticipation). If our greatest desire is to be like Jesus, heaven will be the fulfillment of that desire. "We know that, when he shall appear, we shall be like him; for we shall see him as he is" (1 John 3:2). When we know that fact, and crave its fulfillment with a real urgency, we can view our entry into heaven, whether by death or by the Rapture, as the crowning day. Today could be that crowning day!

Memorize the following verses: Titus 2:13; 1 John 3:2, 3; Revelation 3:11.

Lay Aside Every Weight

The joy of anticipating heaven, the blessed hope of the Second Coming—these realities should transform every part of our daily choices and activities. If Jesus "for the joy that was set before him endured the cross" (Hebrews 12:2), certainly the joy of heaven set before us will give strength for anything we are called upon to face. And it will help us run the race with patience, laying aside every sin that so easily entangles (v. 1).

This should be the true motivation for righteous living. Too many Christians find their motivation for holy living in the legalism that proclaims right actions, but for wrong reasons. Once we have grasped the blessed hope of the Second Coming and the eternal fellowship with our Friend, Jesus, our hatred for sin will be more intense and our motivation for holy living will be what it should be. "Wherefore, beloved, seeing that ye look for such things, be diligent that ye may be found of him in peace, without spot, and blameless" (2 Peter 3:14).

Students of the Future

Futurism is the fad of the day. People seek out astrologers, fortune-tellers, and other predictors of the future in an attempt to see what tomorrow may hold. Such curiosity opens the door for Satan to gain a foothold.

The study of Bible prophecy is right and proper. Yet it should be studied for the proper reason—not for curiosity's sake, but for edification. God's plan for the end times includes far more than the Second Coming. We ought to study the prophecies of these coming events so that we will be better men and women as the hour approaches.

Chapter 8 includes an outline chart of the commonly accepted sequence of events following the rapture of the Church. Some scholars disagree strongly with dispensational interpretations of end-time prophecies, maintaining that the evidence is not strong enough for such a definitive statement on Daniel's 70th week, the judgments, and the new heavens and the new earth. But these same scholars fail to suggest any other chronology.

If there should be error revealed at the time when we see all things clearly, it will not be critical unless we have contended in an unchristian manner for the interpretations we have held. But without such a time line as that presented in the previous chapter, most lay students of the Bible would have difficulty understanding the events that are so obviously recorded in Biblical prophecy. Encourage the adults you teach to be students of Bible prophecy, but to be such with humility and tolerance.

* * * * *

Is the promise of the Second Coming a blessed hope for you and for your students? With God's help, you can make it a vital reality that revolutionizes an otherwise mundane Christian experience. Lord, may it be so!

10

The Church—Doctrine on Display

Our study of the four cardinal doctrines of the Assemblies of God has treated each truth as a separate entity. Yet they belong together like the four sides of a sturdy building. We cannot emphasize one doctrine to the neglect of the other three. We must be Christians who believe and practice the full gospel, or the entire message of the good news.

Although we may believe doctrine in the solitude of the mind, we must also put it into practice, or live it out, in the presence of believers who value and love the same truths that mean so much to us. So it is that the Church, or the body of believers who serve the same Lord, plays such an important part in God's dealings with the human race.

The Church is doctrinal truth on display. It is made up of all who have received the salvation provided through Christ's death on the cross. The official beginning of the New Testament Church is placed at the Day of Pentecost; since that time the Holy Spirit has had special ministries to the entire Church as well as to individual believers. The Church and its ministries are divinely appointed by God as channels by which we receive healing as well as many of the other blessings promised throughout Scripture. Finally, Christ will return for His bride, the Church without spot or wrinkle.

The Church Invisible

The Greek word *ekklesia* or "church" means "the called-out group." In its largest sense it refers to the invisible Church or the redeemed from all ages, both living and dead. In a more specific sense, it is a local congregation of believers who meet together as the organization through which Christ works to edify and perfect the saints and to reach the lost in a geographical location. The Bible uses three illustrations of the invisible Church to help us understand the significant truths of the universal union of all believers in Jesus.

The Bride of Christ

Jesus himself is called the Bridegroom in John 3:29 and Matthew 25:6. The Church as the bride of Christ is now being prepared to become the wife of the Lamb at the great marriage in heaven (Revelation 19:7). After this marriage there will be no separation or divorce. The bride will forever be with her bridegroom (1 Thessalonians 4:17).

This figure for the Church carries special meaning for each Christian. It portrays the intimate union and communion between God and His people. Many religions of the world describe their gods as cruel tyrants or vindictive judges. Even some adherents of Christianity view God as a gruff disciplinarian who continually makes demands of people. But the message of the Bible is that God is love. The illustration of the Church as the bride of Christ is a beautiful vehicle for this truth.

The Body of Christ

The invisible Church is a living organism, not an organization. Each member of the Church, along with Jesus

Christ as the Head, is vitalized by the same divine power, the indwelling Holy Spirit. "And he [Jesus] is the head of the body, the church" (Colossians 1:18). "It is from the Head that the whole body, with all its joints and ligaments, receives its supplies, and thus knit together grows according to God's design" (Colossians 2:19, *NEB).*

By a living union with Christ, each believer is bound together in one organism—the Church—in sharing and manifesting the love and grace of Jesus Christ. Each member of this body, no matter how humble, isolated, or obscure, has a function in this great organism.

The Temple of God

The illustration of the invisible Church as a building that God himself inhabits emphasizes another truth essential to understanding the relationship of the Church to Jesus Christ. "You are built upon the foundation laid by the apostles and prophets, and Christ Jesus himself is the foundation-stone. In him the whole building is bonded together and grows into a holy temple in the Lord. In him you too are being built with all the rest into a spiritual dwelling for God" (Ephesians 2:20-22, *NEB).*

God is everywhere. But He also dwells in His children through whom He manifests His very real presence to the rest of the world. In addition to His special residence in the Church as a temple, He dwells in the temple of each individual Christian (1 Corinthians 3:16, 17; 6:19).

The universal Church is the bride of Christ, the body of Christ, and the temple of God. The love relationship, the life-sustaining principle, and the actual indwelling presence are all essential truths concerning the relationship of the Church to Jesus Christ.

The Local Believers Assembled

The opportunities of modern technology and mass

communication permit gospel outreach in a way never before known, but the New Testament concept of a local church requires some form of assembling with other Christians for worship and edification.

Standards of Membership

Those who identify themselves officially with the local congregation should be born-again Christians. If they have not yet received the special infilling of the Holy Spirit as described in the New Testament, they should certainly understand and subscribe to this cardinal doctrine of Pentecostal belief. They should cooperate wholeheartedly with the ministries of the group to which they belong, for any discord or failure to cooperate hinders the work of the assembly as well as the work of Christ on earth.

Members of a local church have an obligation to maintain a high moral standard before the world. This does not mean that all believers are perfect, but they should be progressing toward the Christlike pattern set before every Christian. An attitude of humility, a contrite heart, and an intense desire to please Christ in all things will produce church members who, though not perfect, can serve as "the light of the world" and "the salt of the earth." The way each member lives is a demonstration of the reality of the doctrinal truths we've been studying.

Cooperation for More Effective Witness

The work of the local church is to preach the message of salvation, to provide spiritual and group fellowship, and to lead believers in worship and service to God. Some people feel that they can accomplish these purposes more effectively in their own associations apart from the local church. But not so! The Word underscores the importance of assembling as the body of Christ: "Let us consider one another to provoke unto love and to good works: not forsaking the assembling of ourselves together, as the manner of some is; but exhorting one another: and so much the more, as ye see the day approaching" (Hebrews 10:24, 25).

The mission of the Church is to make God known to men and women. This mission is best fulfilled when one believer witnesses to one unbeliever about the love and grace of God. Evangelistic outreach is most effective, however, when personal witnessing in the community is a shared responsibility with other members of the Body and a common joy and challenge fostered by the assembled church. The encouragement that comes to the individual through a joint effort results in more effective witnessing and outreach.

The Ordinances of the Church

An ordinance is a divinely established religious custom or practice that is viewed as essential to the fulfillment of spiritual duties. In some churches, as many as seven ordinances are recognized. Evangelicals, however, limit the number of ordinances to those established by Jesus and existing in the practices of the Church since New Testament times. The two Biblical ordinances of the Church are water baptism and Holy Communion.

Memorize the following verses: Matthew 28:19; 1 Corinthians 11:23-26; Ephesians 1:22, 23; 5:25-27; Hebrews 10:24, 25.

Water Baptism

The ordinance of water baptism is administered only once. As the new convert participates in the rite, he announces to all who see or hear of the baptism that a new life in Jesus Christ has begun and that it is the intent of the baptized Christian to follow Christ in complete obedience from that time on.

The method of water baptism. Pentecostal believers almost unanimously practice immersion as the correct form of water baptism and regard all other forms as unscriptural. There are many traditions followed by other churches, but the Bible rather than tradition should be our pattern. Sprinkling and infant baptism are two practices that Pentecostals oppose because they are based on human tradition rather than on scriptural authority.

There are Christians who immerse the candidate three times (triune immersion)—once in the name of the Father, once in the name of the Son, and once in the name of the Holy Ghost. We believe, however, that triune immersion is an error caused by a misinterpretation of the command of Scripture and the meaning of the rite. Since baptism signifies identification with Christ's death, burial, and resurrection, single immersion is sufficient.

The candidate for water baptism. Any believer who sincerely repents of his sins and exercises a living faith in Jesus Christ is eligible for baptism. Infants, of course, have no sins of which to repent. Nor can they exercise the faith that requires understanding the way of salvation and responding to the saving work of Christ. For these reasons, we do not consider infants to be eligible candidates for the ordinance of water baptism.

The symbolism of water baptism. Water baptism is a simple object lesson portraying the fundamentals of the gospel. The submersion beneath the water speaks of Christ's death and burial. The raising of the convert symbolizes Christ's resurrection and victory over death. The participation of the candidate in this symbolic ritual emphasizes his spiritual identification with Christ and His work. Paul speaks of being "buried with him in baptism, wherein also ye are risen with him" (Colossians 2:12).

The importance of water baptism. Water baptism is an outward sign of an inward work. In itself it has no saving power. People are baptized because they are saved, not in order to be saved. Although baptism is not absolutely essential to salvation, it is essential to full obedience. As Peter preached on the Day of Pentecost, he charged his listeners: "Repent, and be baptized every one of you in the name of Jesus Christ for the remission of sins, and ye shall receive the gift of the Holy Ghost" (Acts 2:38). Both actions—to repent and to be baptized—are commands that every obedient believer will fulfill.

The Lord's Supper

The Lord's Supper or Holy Communion was instituted by Jesus on the eve of His crucifixion. The ordinance is a memorial of Christ's death. The bread represents His broken body, and the wine represents His shed blood.

Origin of the ordinance. The Lord's Supper in the New Covenant took the place of the Passover in the Old Testament law. It was while Jesus and the disciples were celebrating the Passover meal that the Communion ritual was instituted. On that night before the Crucifixion, the 13 men were recalling the events of Israel's deliverance from Egypt. Taking up the bread and the wine that were on the table, Jesus gave each a special significance in the redemptive work He was about to do.

"And as they were eating, Jesus took bread, and blessed it, and brake it, and gave it to the disciples, and said, Take, eat; this is my body. And he took the cup, and gave thanks, and gave it to them, saying, Drink ye all of it; for this is my blood of the new testament, which is shed for many for the remission of sins" (Matthew 26:26-28).

The frequency of the memorial. Paul told the Corinthians: "As often as ye eat this bread, and drink this cup, ye do show the Lord's death till he come" (1 Corinthians 11:26). How often should we commemorate the death of our Lord in this manner? Is there a good basis for celebrating the Lord's Supper once a month?

The Bible gives no directive on the matter of frequency. It seems appropriate, therefore, to observe the memorial frequently enough that we are regularly reminded of the atoning work of Jesus Christ. On the other hand, it should not be observed so often that the act becomes routine and commonplace. Many evangelicals have concluded that once a month provides a proper balance between familiarity and remembering, with the possibility of observing Communion on other special occasions as well.

The significance of Communion. The ordinance of the Lord's Supper is such a solemn and important ceremony that persons participating are given special warning to prepare themselves for the holy occasion. "Whosoever shall eat this bread, and drink this cup of the Lord, unworthily, shall be guilty of the body and blood of the Lord" (1 Corinthians 11:27).

This caution should not frighten a Christian into abstaining from Holy Communion. The command to partake is still valid. "But let a man examine himself, and so let him eat of that bread, and drink of that cup" (1 Corinthians 11:28). Partaking of the Lord's Supper reminds us that our experience of salvation must be kept current; the Christian life is a spiritual walk in which we must continually open our hearts for cleansing.

The Lord's Supper reminds us of Christ's atoning work at Calvary. It looks forward to the Second Coming when our salvation will be perfect and complete. But this ordinance also points to another of the cardinal doctrines we have been studying: divine healing.

The abuse Jesus endured in His body as He purchased our salvation on the cross was for our physical healing as well as our spiritual restoration. "He was wounded for our transgressions, he was bruised for our iniquities: the chastisement of our peace was upon him; and with his stripes we are healed" (Isaiah 53:5). The receiving of the Lord's Supper is an excellent time to reach out in faith for the healing that the believer may need.

The termination of the ordinance. The keeping of the Lord's Supper, like the rite of water baptism, will end with the coming of the Lord for His saints. Paul's command is to remember the Lord's death, through Holy Communion, until Jesus comes (1 Corinthians 11:26). These ordinances are for a testimony now. They are symbols of the reality of our salvation, our healing, and the return of Jesus for His bride.

We Hold These Truths

The great truths of Scripture and of the Assemblies of God have been surveyed. But like all doctrine, they must be taught and translated into living reality, into Christian commitments and life-styles that reflect a deep belief that Jesus Christ is our Saviour, our Healer, the Giver of the Holy Spirit, and our soon-to-return King.

Too many Christians live, however, as though these doctrinal truths are superfluous or unnecessary. "As long as I know Jesus as my Saviour, I'll get to heaven, and that's all that is important. I'll leave the details of doctrine to someone else." This attitude is dangerous. God expects spiritual growth of every Christian. He commands us to move on to maturity in understanding and experience. "Let us leave the elementary teachings about Christ and go on to maturity" (Hebrews 6:1, *NIV*). To stop with the foundation of salvation, failing to build the spiritual edifice God desires, displeases God and is actual disobedience if we refuse to press on toward the maturity that these truths present to us.

Sunday school teachers especially should be well versed in the Word and in the doctrines based on that Word. But the challenge to learn the weightier truths and principles of the Word demands time and effort that too many Christians are unwilling to expend. Saturday night's quick reading of the next day's lesson will not produce the kind of teachers the Sunday school needs. It can be said of them as the writer of Hebrews said concerning some people in his day: "Though by this time you ought to be teachers, you need someone to teach you the ABC of God's oracles over again" (Hebrews 5:12, *NEB*).

A teacher is not necessarily a person who stands in front of a class of students. He is a person who has learned himself and can share that knowledge and experience at whatever level the students may be.

We Hold These Truths Steadfastly

Paul used a vivid image to describe the person who has not settled in his own mind the doctrinal truth that leads to Christian maturity: ". . . tossed to and fro, and carried about with every wind of doctrine" (Ephesians 4:14). The person who wavers in his own thinking, leaving the fundamentals that have been passed down by Spirit-anointed and Bible-believing teachers, is like a boat without a guiding rudder. He follows after each new book, theological fad, or religious idea that comes along.

Paul was very much concerned that his converts and young spiritual leaders were well-grounded in the Word and its doctrine or teaching. To Timothy he said, "Watch your life and doctrine closely. Persevere in them" (1

Timothy 4:16, *NIV)*. To the Thessalonians he urged, "Stand firm and hold to the teachings we passed on to you, whether by word of mouth or by letter" (2 Thessalonians 2:15, *NIV)*. The same urgent plea for steadfastness in doctrine and profession is repeated in the Book of Hebrews: "Let us hold fast our profession" (4:14); and, "Let us hold fast the profession of our faith without wavering" (10:23).

We Teach These Truths Diligently

We are to hold the doctrine without wavering for two good reasons: to help those who are sincerely searching and to have an answer for those who rebel against and reject the pure doctrine. An elder, according to Titus 1:9, "must hold firmly to the trustworthy message as it has been taught, so that he can encourage others by sound doctrine and refute those who oppose it" *(NIV)*.

To Timothy, Paul spoke stern words of responsibility for his task as pastor-teacher: "If you point these things out to the brothers, you will be a good minister of Christ Jesus, brought up in the truths of the faith and of the good teaching that you have followed" (1 Timothy 4:6, *NIV)*. Again to Titus Paul said, "You must teach what is in accord with sound doctrine" (Titus 2:1, *NIV)*.

* * * * *

This study of the cardinal doctrines of Scripture and of the Assemblies of God has been a brief survey based on the key verses of Scripture relating to each basic truth. But there is more detail to be uncovered and shared with students or with Christian friends who are new in the way. Study the Scriptures diligently, making all of its Books and passages part of your doctrinal equipment.

"All scripture is given by inspiration of God, and is profitable for doctrine, for reproof, for correction, for instruction in righteousness: that the man of God may be perfect, thoroughly furnished unto all good works" (2 Timothy 3:16, 17).

Suggested Reading

Bosworth, F.F. *Christ the Healer: Messages on Divine Healing*. Old Tappan, NJ: Fleming H. Revell Co., n.d.

Gee, Donald. *The Fruit of the Spirit*. Springfield, MO: Gospel Publishing House, reprinted 1975.

Gee, Donald. *Fruitful or Barren?* Springfield, MO: Gospel Publishing House, 1961.

Holdcroft, L. Thomas. *Divine Healing: A Comparative Study*. Springfield, MO: Gospel Publishing House, 1967.

Horton, Harold. *The Gifts of the Spirit*. Springfield, MO: Gospel Publishing House, U.S. ed. 1975.

Horton, Stanley M. *The Promise of His Coming*. Springfield, MO: Gospel Publishing House, 1967.

Horton, Stanley M. *What the Bible Says About the Holy Spirit*. Springfield, MO: Gospel Publishing House, 1976.

Jeter, Hugh. *By His Stripes: The Doctrine of Divine Healing*. Springfield, MO: Gospel Publishing House, 1977.

Nelson, P.C. *Bible Doctrines*. Springfield, MO: Gospel Publishing House, rev. 1971.

Pearlman, Myer. *Knowing the Doctrines of the Bible*. Springfield, MO: Gospel Publishing House, 1937.

Riggs, Ralph M. *We Believe*. Springfield, MO: Gospel Publishing House, 1954.

Sanderson, John W. *The Fruit of the Spirit.* Grand Rapids: Zondervan Publishing House, 1976.

Position Papers

Divine Healing: An Integral Part of the Gospel. Springfield, MO: Gospel Publishing House, 1974.

Inerrancy of Scripture, The. Springfield, MO: Gospel Publishing House, 1976.

Statement of Fundamental Truths. Springfield, MO: Gospel Publishing House.